The Art of Self-Discipline

Practical Techniques to Boost Mental Toughness, Crush Bad Habits, and Resist Temptations to (Finally) Achieve Your Goals, without Self-Sabotage

Logan Mind

Download Your Free Book!... 6

© COPYRIGHT 2024 - ALL RIGHTS RESERVED. 7

How to Download Your Extras.. 8

Other Books 10

Join my Review Team!.. 12

Introduction 13

Chapter 1: Understanding Self-Discipline.. 16

Chapter 2: The Foundation of Mental Toughness................................ 26

Chapter 3: Identifying and Overcoming Bad Habits 35

Chapter 4: Resisting Temptations Effectively...................................... 45

Chapter 5: Goal Setting and Achievement 56

Chapter 6: Time Management for Self-Discipline................................ 68

Chapter 7: Developing a Disciplined Mindset...................................... 80

Chapter 8: Building Resilience and Grit... 92

Chapter 9: The Role of Physical Health in Self-Discipline 102

Chapter 10: Emotional Regulation and Self-Discipline 113

Chapter 11: Productivity Techniques for the Disciplined Mind 124

Chapter 12: Overcoming Procrastination 135

Chapter 13: Maintaining Long-Term Self-Discipline 146

To Conclude 157

Other Books 160

Help Me! 161

Join my Review Team! 162

EMOTIONAL INTELLIGENCE
for Social Success

FREE DOWNLOAD: pxl.to/loganmindfreebook

LOGAN MIND

EXTRAS

https://pxl.to/LoganMind

Books
Workbooks
FREE GIFTS
Review Team
Audiobooks
Contacts

CLICK NOW!

@loganmindpsychology

Download Your Free Book!

As a way of saying thanks for your purchase, I'm offering the book **Emotional Intelligence** for Social Success for FREE to you, my reader.

Inside the book, you'll **discover** a wealth of valuable information. You'll learn techniques to **improve** your social interactions and strategies to **manage** your emotions effectively. You'll also pick up tips on developing **empathy** and understanding, gain insights into building stronger **relationships**, and learn methods to handle social **challenges** with ease.

If you want to **boost** your emotional intelligence and succeed in social environments, make sure to grab this free book. It's a game-changer!

To get instant **access**, just head over to:

https://pxl.to/loganmindfreebook

Don't miss out on this opportunity to enhance your social skills and emotional intelligence. Get your free copy now!

© COPYRIGHT 2024 - ALL RIGHTS RESERVED.

The content contained within this book may not be reproduced, duplicated or transmitted without direct written permission from the author or the publisher. Under no circumstances will any blame or legal responsibility be held against the publisher, or author, for any damages, reparation, or monetary loss due to the information contained within this book, either directly or indirectly.

LEGAL NOTICE:

This book is copyright protected. It is only for personal use.

You cannot amend, distribute, sell, use, quote or paraphrase any part, or the content within this book, without the consent of the author or publisher.

How to Download Your Extras

You're about to embark on a **transformative** journey to unparalleled self-discipline with some awesome resources that come with this book. Why miss out on specialized tools that are proven to boost your understanding and mastery of self-discipline right from the get-go? Unlock these extras to supercharge your personal **growth** and set yourself up for success in everything you do.

Let's dive into why these extras are must-haves:

First up, you've got a **downloadable** and practical PDF 21-Day Challenge designed to kickstart your efforts. It's packed with structured actions and tips spread over three weeks. This gem, usually priced at $14.99, ensures you're not just reading about self-discipline—you're living it.

Next, there's the 101+ Inspiring Quotes on Self-Discipline. It's like having a pocket-sized **motivation** station wherever you go. Sprinkle your daily routine with words of wisdom from the world's greatest minds on discipline to keep your spirits high and your eyes on the prize.

Then there's the Quick Habit-Breaking **Checklist**—worth $9.99—perfect for spotting and squashing those pesky negative habits. Start breaking cycles like a pro with this streamlined, actionable guide that shows you effective techniques to clear your path.

As if that wasn't enough, you'll also snag an insightful bonus worth $14.99: Emotional Intelligence for Social Success. This will help you develop emotional regulation and social **skills** to complement your self-discipline game and really round out your approach.

Adding these goodies to your toolkit will arm you with everything you need to get the most out of your self-discipline journey, and they're just a quick **download** away.

Check out the extras here:

https://pxl.to/6-taos-lm-extras

Other Books

You're holding a **powerful tool** in your hands, designed to help you master **self-discipline** and achieve your goals without self-sabotage. But why stop there? To truly expand your understanding and improve your life holistically, it's crucial to complement this read with other insightful resources.

I've also authored books that dive into interconnected realms of **personal development** that'll undoubtedly boost your current knowledge. These books have either hit the shelves already or are about to make their debut.

Think of this book as just the kickoff for your **self-improvement** journey. To help you build on the ideas presented here, why not check out:

• An eye-opening guide on Emotional Intelligence Habits. This book gives you practical techniques for understanding and managing your emotions like a pro.

• A journey into boosting your Self-Esteem, which ties right into your ability to keep up the discipline and perseverance you're aiming for.

• In a soon-to-be-released addition, you'll uncover techniques designed to elevate your mind through Brain Training, helping you harness your **cognitive prowess** to outthink obstacles and stay laser-focused.

Ready to dive in? Here's what you need to do:

• Follow the link below

- Click on All My Books

- Grab the ones that catch your eye

- If you want to get in touch with me, you'll find all my contact info at the end of the link

Check out all my books and contacts here:

https://pxl.to/LoganMind

Join my Review Team!

Thank you so much for reading my **book**! Your support means the world to me. If you're an **avid reader** and love to share your thoughts, I've got a special offer just for you. How would you like to snag a **free copy** of my latest book in exchange for your honest feedback? Your **review** could really help me grow and improve my work, and I'd be over the moon for your input.

Getting on board the ARC team is a piece of cake:

• Hit the link or scan the QR code

• Click on the **book cover** on the page that pops up

• Tap on "Join Review Team"

• Sign up to BookSprout

• Get a heads up every time I drop a new **book**

Want to check out the **team**? Here's where you can find us:

https://pxl.to/loganmindteam

So, what do you say? Ready to dive in and be part of this awesome **reading** adventure? Your thoughts could make all the difference!

Introduction

Have you ever **wondered** why some people seem to have this magical ability to resist temptation and stick to their goals effortlessly? You see it all the time. You know, the ones who wake up at the crack of dawn to hit the gym, who power through their to-do lists without getting sidetracked by the latest trending YouTube video. I've spent years diving into what makes the human mind tick, and let me tell you—it's fascinating stuff.

So, you're sitting here with this book, probably because you want to get a handle on this thing we call **self-discipline**. Maybe you're sick of falling back into the same old habits or procrastinating until the last minute. Guess what? I get it. I've been there too, slogging through those murky waters where you'd rather just hit snooze instead of tackling those big dreams.

Let's get one thing straight: there's no magic wand, no quick-fix fairy tale. But—and it's a big but—the **strategies** packed into this book? They can help you transform. We'll explore the nuts and bolts of self-control, backed not just by psychology, but by some solid neuroscience too. See, self-discipline isn't just some abstract concept. It's like a muscle you can train, just like your biceps or your brain.

When I sat down to write this book, I wanted to offer more than just fluffy advice. I wanted practical **techniques** and actionable steps to help you master self-discipline. Stuff you can start using today to see changes. And believe me, as someone who's had a fair share of wins and flops in the journey of personal development, I'm speaking from experience.

Ever hammer away at a goal, only to watch it crumble under the pressures of life? Yeah, same here. Turns out, **willpower** can get worn out like an old pair of sneakers. This book? It's your guide to managing that willpower fatigue. Think of it like learning to pace yourself in a marathon—keeping energy for the long haul so each step gets you closer, not burning out halfway through.

Now, let's talk mental toughness. Another fancy term, sure, but vital. Mental toughness isn't just for Navy SEALs or Olympic athletes—it's something you can tap into every single day. Imagine building **resilience** like you'd build a house, brick by brick. This book looks at those bricks—emotional intelligence, mental resilience, and the right mindset—and helps you start laying them down.

Bad **habits**? Oh, we all have 'em. Recognizing the lousy patterns in your life is the first step. And boy, breaking those habits feels like trying to untangle a year's worth of Christmas lights. But, we're not just untangling here; we're replacing those knots with bright, new strands of positive behaviors. Techniques, practical exercises—these pages are loaded with tools to help you fix those habits.

Let me ask you something—how often do temptations knock on your door? Like when your phone pings and, suddenly, you find yourself scrolling away precious hours? Resisting such temptations ain't easy, but it's doable. This book delves into strategies for impulse control and environmental tweaks to help keep distractions at bay. Small changes add up to big wins, right?

And **goals**—oh, let's dig into that. Setting them, chasing them, and most importantly, smashing through obstacles. It's not just about aiming high, but aligning those goals with what's genuinely meaningful to you. By the time you're flipping through, you'll be knee-deep in frameworks and practical exercises designed to turn lofty aspirations into achievable steps.

Ever felt swamped by time, like there's never enough of it? Welcome to the club. Balancing responsibilities, hobbies, personal time—it's chaos. But here's where time management becomes your best buddy. This book lays out how to prioritize, focus, and eliminate those sneaky time-wasters. Start with simple techniques, and you'll see big shifts in how effectively you can power through your day.

One last thing, since we're getting real here: your mind. Pushing beyond perceived limits and overcoming self-limiting beliefs can be game-changers. Your inner dialogue can either push you forward or pull you back, and you'll dive into practices to sculpt a disciplined mindset.

I'm all about the big picture, too. Long-term resilience and grit? That stuff manifests through consistent effort, by bouncing back after setbacks, and keeping your head in the game when everything seems to fall apart.

How does your health fit into all this? It's crucial. Nutrition, exercise, sleep—a balanced body nurtures a disciplined mind. The connection is real, and I'll show you how making shifts in your physical well-being pays off in mega dividends for your goals.

And emotions, let's not overlook them. Regulating your emotions plays a huge role in self-discipline. Your ability to keep those feelings in check and use them as motivation shifts everything.

Ending here, whether you're aiming to unlock that holy grail of productivity or chasing that big dream—self-discipline cuts across every goal. And, in this book, I'm sharing the map. Ready to reshape your life? Dive in. Let's go on this journey together.

Chapter 1: Understanding Self-Discipline

Ever felt like you're **wrestling** with yourself to get stuff done? One minute you're ready to conquer the world, the next you're binging on your favorite show. It's a pull, a constant tug-of-war. But what if you could change that by understanding self-discipline?

In this chapter, we'll dive into the why and how of **self-control**. Ever wondered why some folks seem to have endless willpower? It's not magic. It's just the **brain** working its wonders, and guess what? You can make it work for you too.

We'll chat about the **habits** that shape us. You know, those little actions that seem small but pack a serious punch over time. Plus, we'll tackle the slippery slope of giving up when you're tired – yep, **willpower** fatigue is real, and managing it is key.

By the end of this chapter, you'll start to see self-discipline in a new light. You'll get a good grip on how your **mind** works and how you can steer it better. Ready to peek behind the **curtain**? Let's go!

You'll discover the ins and outs of self-discipline, unraveling the **mysteries** of why some days you're unstoppable and others you can barely get off the couch. We'll explore the science behind willpower and how you can harness it to your advantage. You'll learn about the power of small, consistent actions and how they can snowball into life-changing results.

Don't worry if you've struggled with self-discipline before. This chapter will give you the tools to understand your own behavior and make lasting changes. You'll find out how to work with your brain instead of against it, making self-discipline feel less like a chore and more like a superpower.

So, buckle up and get ready to transform your approach to getting things done. By the time you finish this chapter, you'll be armed with knowledge and strategies to take control of your actions and steer your life in the direction you want. Let's unlock the secrets of self-discipline together!

The Psychology of Self-Control

You might think of **self-control** as being able to deal with your thoughts, emotions, and actions to get to the end result you want. It's like managing the little voice in your head that says, "One more cookie won't hurt," when you're trying to stick to a diet. So, it's less about absolute restraint and more about guiding yourself towards long-term goals.

When diving into how your **brain** makes decisions and controls impulses, it gets really interesting. We're talking about a mental process that happens in the front part of your brain, called the prefrontal cortex. This part is super important for planning and self-regulation. It's like the brain's CEO, making executive decisions, forming strategies, and saying "no" to tempting but bad options.

But let's take a step back. How exactly does this brainy CEO work with self-control? It's all about neural pathways and signals. Imagine pressing the brakes when driving—this is similar to what your brain does to stop impulsive behaviors. When you're tempted to binge-watch shows right before a final exam, your prefrontal cortex works to keep you on track, focusing on what matters most in the long haul.

Ever wondered why some **decisions** are so hard? Your brain is actually battling it out, impulse versus reason. And guess who's there trying to referee? That front part of your brain again. Looking at a slice of cake, the primitive part of your brain screams "Eat it!" But the prefrontal cortex steps in, reminding you of your long-term health goals or weight loss plan.

Sometimes, though, the referee doesn't always win. If you're low on sleep or stressed, your brain's "brakes" get a little rusty. Managing impulses becomes harder as your mental energy depletes. It's like trying to study after pulling an all-nighter—things get messy. The less energy and focus you have, the harder it is to resist those everyday **temptations**.

So how can you help your trusty brain stay strong in matters of self-control? Well, setting clear **goals** can be one way. When you know exactly what your goals are, it becomes easier for your brain to align your actions with them. You're giving your prefrontal cortex clear marching orders. If it knows what's happening and maintains focus, you're more likely to stay on track.

Believe it or not, **habits** also play into this. Creating routine behaviors can make it so your brain has less work to do. Optimize your environment. If you set predictable, positive patterns, your brain won't need to process difficult decisions over and over. Want to eat healthy? Keep junk food out of the house.

Sometimes it helps to **visualize** success too. Not to get all dreamy or anything, but if you imagine yourself achieving your goal, your brain gets a sneak peek at the rewards. This can strengthen your self-discipline by making the end result look real and within reach. Concrete visual goals can add motivation, driving behavior aligned with these targets.

Don't just aim for perfection—understand it's about **progress** and making better choices incrementally. Remember, it's all in the way you manage your daily decisions, which roll up into your bigger goals. Stay mindful of this connection, and you'll notice a reinforcement of self-control across various aspects of life.

And so, that's a look into how the psychology of self-control plays into managing your thoughts, emotions, and actions. It's a continuous cycle of making decisions influenced by your brain's unique workings and the smart intervention of your prefrontal cortex. Amazing how understanding this one area can provide insight into improving your self-discipline, bit by bit.

Neuroscience and Self-Discipline

Let's dive into how your **brain** works when it comes to self-discipline. It's pretty fascinating stuff. Your brain has this cool thing called dopamine, which is like nature's **motivation** fuel. When you accomplish something you like, your brain releases dopamine, making you feel awesome. This feeling pushes you to do more of these things. It's like when you nail a test and can't wait to tell everyone about it.

But here's the catch. This same system can make self-discipline tricky. Your brain **rewards** you for quick wins, which aren't always the best ones. Binge-watching shows, endless social media scrolling, snacking on junk food – these all give you quick dopamine hits. You end up craving these easy rewards instead of tackling tougher tasks. That's where your struggle with self-discipline kicks in.

Now, let's talk about something called neuroplasticity. It means your brain can actually change and adapt. Cool, right? If you keep doing an action over and over, certain **pathways** in your brain get stronger. It's like walking the same route until a clear path forms. This applies to **habits** too. The more often you do something, the easier it gets because the pathway is better established. This neuroplasticity magic means you can teach your brain to support better habits. Want to start exercising? Begin with a little each day. Your brain will catch on and make it easier to keep at it over time.

But here's where things get messy: **stress**. It does a number on your brain. When you're stressed, your brain goes into survival mode. It hijacks the part of your brain responsible for self-control – the prefrontal cortex. When you're stressing out, making rational decisions and sticking to your goals becomes really tough.

Stress floods your brain with cortisol. This hormone helps you deal with real danger, but in everyday life? It's mostly a roadblock. You're likely to slip back into bad habits, seeking those easy dopamine rewards we talked about earlier. Eating junk food or binging shows feels right in those tense moments. Your brain's wiring pushes you that way under stress.

So, what can you do? Keep the stress monster in check where you can. Develop some methods to stay calm – mindfulness, light exercise, chatting with friends. These strategies reduce cortisol levels and help you regain control over that precious prefrontal cortex.

In a nutshell, understanding how your brain handles **discipline** reveals why it's harder to resist temptations today than it was to feel motivated by that pep talk last week. Knowing this helps you work those brain circuits in your favor, turning self-discipline from something that nags into something that sticks.

Sounds more doable now, doesn't it? Small wins – guarding your brain's rewarding habits, fine-tuning neuroplastic moments, and riding out stress – keep those dopamine-driven reactions in check.

So there you have it. No fancy jargon, no highbrow brain stuff here. Just real talk on your brain and **self-discipline**.

The Role of Habits in Self-Discipline

Habits are like your brain's way of hitting the "easy" button. When you do something regularly, it becomes second nature. That's because your brain loves to conserve **energy** for more important stuff. Think about brushing your teeth. You don't even think about it—you just do it. That's a **habit** in action. And this automatic behavior can save you a ton of mental energy, which will help you stay disciplined.

But how do habits become automatic in the first place? Well, it has a lot to do with a part of your brain called the basal ganglia. This part handles repetitive tasks and turns them into habits over time. So, when you **practice** something regularly, your basal ganglia takes over, making that action easier and more automatic. It's like building a mental shortcut.

Now, you might wonder how you can tie these automatic actions to bigger goals. Enter habit **stacking**. Basically, when you pair a new habit with an existing one, you can piggyback on that existing mental shortcut. Think of it as connecting new pathways in your brain to older, more well-trodden ones. For instance, if you always have a cup of coffee in the morning, you could make it a habit to review your daily goals while sipping that coffee. Simple, right?

It's all about making small, incremental changes that your brain won't reject outright. Don't aim to overhaul your entire **routine** in one shot—that's a surefire way to get overwhelmed. Plus, your brain is likely to resist big changes because they consume more mental energy. Tiny adjustments work better because they're manageable. And once they become habits, they free up mental space for other things.

Keeping things practical, you could start with simple actions like:

- Doing five minutes of stretching right after you brush your teeth

- Drinking a glass of water as soon as you wake up

- Writing a quick to-do list while your morning coffee brews

What you're doing is setting small but stable anchors in your daily schedule.

When it comes to forming habits, **consistency** is king. Your brain needs repetitive action to turn behaviors into habits. Consider how athletes train. They might spend hours practicing the same move until it becomes second nature. Consistent practice trains the basal ganglia to take over, making these actions almost effortless in the long run.

So, how can you keep up consistency? Simple reminders can work wonders. Setting alarms, sticky notes, or even using habit-tracking apps helps ensure you won't forget. The key is not to miss two days in a row because a break makes it harder to jump back in. New habits are fragile—they need regular attention before they become rooted.

Another thing to recognize is the role of **rewards**. These can be tiny—like giving yourself a small treat or taking a couple of minutes to relax after completing your task. Rewards help create positive consequences for your actions, making your brain more likely to repeat them. Think of it as giving your brain a little high-five.

Overall, habits play a massive role in **self-discipline**. They're the automatic pilots of your daily actions, allowing you to coast smoothly through tasks that otherwise would require lots of mental effort. Using strategies like habit stacking can make forming new habits less daunting. Staying consistent and rewarding yourself helps these habits stick, fortifying your self-discipline along the way.

So, take a moment to look at your current habits. Can you stack anything new onto those? Could you make some tiny tweaks for a better routine? The power lies with you.

Willpower Fatigue and Management

Think of **willpower** as a battery. It doesn't stay fully charged forever; it runs out. You wake up chipper and ready to tackle the day, but after a dozen little decisions—or major ones—you start feeling less "bring it on" and more "leave me alone." Your willpower gets tired, just like you do after a long day.

So, what drains this mental battery of yours? **Decisions**, for one. Ever felt worn out after a morning full of meetings, even though you've been sitting down most of the time? That's because every decision, every little choice... it all eats into your willpower. Imagine having to choose what to wear in the morning, deciding on breakfast, or dealing with traffic—each nibbles away at that willpower.

Stress is another biggie. Got something weighing on your mind all day? Maybe a tough work project or personal problem? That's sapping your willpower. Plus, trying to resist temptations—like saying no to that cookie when you're on a diet—chips away at it, too. Throw in a lack of sleep, and you've got yourself a drained battery pretty quick.

So, how do you **manage** that?

For starters, recognize your limits. Pay attention to when your willpower starts flagging. Notice when you're finding decisions tougher to make or when you're more likely to snap at someone—clues that your willpower is nearly spent. By knowing yourself well, you can spot these signs early and take action.

Another way to manage your willpower is to reduce the number of decisions you have to make. Simplify where you can. Wear the same type of clothes every day, have the same breakfast... little things to save that mental energy for the important stuff.

Set **routines** for yourself. Make good habits automatic so you don't have to think about them. Brush your teeth right after getting up. Go for a walk right after lunch. When these things become second nature, they require next to no willpower.

Delegate some decisions to a later time. Tired after a long day? Do you have plans to figure out your meals for the week or to decide on a significant purchase? Push it till the morning when you're likely to be more recharged. It's all about timing.

Something else you can do is give yourself **breaks**. Take a walk, listen to music, catch up on some light reading. These breaks can help refresh your mind, giving you a chance to recharge some of that willpower.

Finally, and perhaps most importantly, it's crucial to know when to seek **help** or use external supports. This might mean having a friend hold you accountable, using a planning tool to keep you organized, or even seeing a mentor. It's about balancing the load, to keep your willpower from running out too soon.

By thinking of willpower as something that isn't infinite, you can find strategies to keep it running smoothly. With awareness and the right tools, you can manage your willpower better, keeping it in reserve for when you need it most.

In Conclusion

This chapter has given you the **basics** of self-discipline. You've explored how your **brain** works, the importance of **habits**, and even the concept of **willpower**. With a better understanding of these concepts, you're on your way to mastering self-control and achieving your **goals**. To help you remember the main points, here are the key takeaways:

Your **self-control** is all about managing your thoughts, emotions, and actions to reach long-term goals. Your brain plays a big role in self-discipline, especially the prefrontal cortex. Making good habits is crucial because they save energy and help you stay disciplined. **Willpower** can get tired, just like a muscle, so it's important to manage it wisely. Knowing when you're running low on willpower can help you plan and take breaks before you get too **exhausted**.

You now have some powerful tools to tackle **challenges** and stay on track with your goals. Apply what you've learned, and you'll see great results. Believe in yourself and keep striving for that self-discipline. You've got what it takes to succeed!

Chapter 2: The Foundation of Mental Toughness

Ever **wondered** why some folks seem rock solid no matter what life throws at them? I've often asked myself the same, grabbing every chance to unravel the secrets behind that **fortitude**. You're probably itching to peel back those layers and discover what makes mental toughness tick, aren't you?

Well, this chapter is your **gateway**. It's not some dry monologue stuffed with jargon. Instead, you'll find tidbits designed to get your gears turning, gently nudging you towards **insights** that could flip the script for you.

We all face **challenges**; I get it. And trust me, diving into the core of mental resilience and tapping into emotional wisdom is a total game-changer. It's the difference between crumbling under pressure and standing tall. This isn't just about surviving—it's about **thriving**.

By exploring emotional smarts and self-control, you'll unlock a bit of that hidden **strength** you might not even know you've got. Seriously, it's like putting together a puzzle, with each piece bringing you closer to a clearer, stronger version of yourself.

Curious about how it all fits together? You'll get a glimpse into the **growth** mindset approach, something I've found personally eye-opening. Ready to dive in? You're about to get hooked...

Defining Mental Toughness

Ever tried sticking with something really tough and staying focused when things get crazy? That's **mental toughness** in a nutshell. It's about holding on tight through challenges and not losing your cool under pressure. Think of it like the backbone of self-discipline. You'll need it to face setbacks and keep pushing toward your goals, no matter what gets thrown your way.

Mental toughness has four main parts, each playing a role in keeping you on track:

Control: This means having a grip on your emotions and actions. You don't let your feelings or outside forces sway you too much. It's like the steering wheel of a car – you need it to steer in the right direction. Lose control, and you might just veer off course. And let's face it, no one wants to be swerving all over the road when they're trying to get somewhere.

Commitment: This is about sticking to your goals and promises. It's the engine that keeps you moving forward. If you commit, you don't give up easily. Simple as that. Whether it's getting up early to hit the gym or dedicating an hour a day to learning a new skill, you're in it for the long haul. Without commitment, you'll find yourself quitting as soon as things get tough.

Challenge: This one's about seeing obstacles as opportunities. Let's say life hands you a lemon. Someone with mental toughness sees it not just as a lemon, but as the chance to make lemonade, or whatever else you fancy. You're open to new experiences, stretch yourself, and aren't afraid to step out of your comfort zone.

Confidence: It's believing in your ability to meet challenges head-on. Confidence gives you the guts to face whatever comes your way. It's the shield that protects you from self-doubt when things are rough. Ever noticed how things go a lot smoother when you believe you can do it? No retreating into a shell – you face your fears.

So how does mental toughness help you reach long-term goals? Life doesn't always go to plan. Sometimes you face setbacks that jolt you right off track. It's like running into a wall. However, with mental toughness, you learn to bounce back instead of giving up. You become a bit like a rubber ball – you hit the ground, but you bounce right back up.

When you harness this bounce-back ability, you're building **resilience**. Let's say you fail an important test. Instead of letting it crush you, you study harder and try again. Eventually, you pass. This not only boosts your confidence but gives you control over your future. And every time you bounce back, you get a bit stronger, a bit tougher.

It's all about playing the long game. Goals worth achieving aren't usually accomplished overnight. They take time, effort, and a whole lot of grit. Mental toughness means you're willing to put in the work, push through the pain, and keep your eyes on the prize.

So, to wrap it up – mental toughness: sticking with challenges, staying cool under pressure, controlling your emotions and actions, committing to your goals, seeing challenges as opportunities, and believing in yourself. With these in your toolbox, you're well-equipped to tackle just about anything that comes your way. Ain't that something worth striving for? I think so.

The Components of Mental Resilience

What exactly is **psychological resilience**? Well, it's your ability to adapt and bounce back when life gets tough. Picture yourself getting knocked down only to stand up stronger. It's like being a tough rubber band – you stretch, bend, and maybe even twist, but you never break. This knack for recovery can make all the difference when you're dealing with **stress** and tackling life's obstacles.

How does this actually happen? It's not magic. It starts with being **flexible** in your thinking. If you're too rigid, any setback can feel like the end of the world. But if you're willing to see challenges from multiple angles, it's easier to find a way out. Imagine life throws you a curveball – instead of panicking, you adapt your strategy. For instance, if you lose your job, rather than seeing it as a disaster, you could view it as a chance to pursue something you're passionate about. Flexibility in thinking isn't about being wishy-washy. It's about being open to change and willing to revise your plans as you go.

Think about it—when you're adaptable, you're better at **problem-solving**. You're like a mechanic with a full toolkit, ready to fix any issue that comes up. Maybe you'll take a detour you didn't plan, but that new route could lead to better opportunities or unexpected insights. Flexibility helps you stay grounded and reduces the stress of navigating life's unexpected twists and turns.

And let's not forget about having a good **support system**. Seriously, try to imagine climbing a mountain entirely on your own—it's lonely and way more difficult. But imagine doing it with a group of friends or supportive colleagues. Everything changes. The climbs are less daunting, and the achievements become sweeter.

Studies show that positive relationships can act as a buffer against stress. They give you a sounding board, a place to vent, and a safety net for when things don't go as planned. Close friends, understanding family, and encouraging mentors lift you up when you're feeling down. They can offer advice, share their own experiences, or simply listen. These interactions often remind you that you're not in this alone.

Nurturing these relationships takes effort, but it's worth it. Spend time with the people who make you feel good about yourself. Engage in activities that bring you closer together. It doesn't matter if it's cooking a meal with a loved one, going for a walk with a friend, or calling someone just to chat. These little moments add up, creating a strong support system that can get you through tough times.

Think about the last time you faced something difficult. Wasn't that sense of **community** or friendship a huge help? Some problems feel smaller when shared. Plus, when people believe in you, it's easier to believe in yourself.

So, flexibility in thinking and strong social bonds – these are just two components that build your **mental resilience**. Picture yourself as that strong rubber band, bending but never breaking, always ready to snap back into shape. That's the power of **mental toughness**, and trust me, you've got everything you need to develop it.

Emotional Intelligence and Self-Discipline

Think of **emotional intelligence** as your superpower to recognize, understand, and manage your emotions. It's like having an emotional radar—you spot feelings as they come, understand them, and manage them in a way that helps you stay **disciplined**.

Imagine waking up for an early morning jog. You're not in the mood, feeling groggy and unmotivated. What if you had the ability to understand that feeling deeply, knowing it'll soon pass once you get going? More importantly, you recognize it but don't let it control your actions. You're better equipped to push through and put on those running shoes. Better still, you're prepared for your brain's early-morning tantrum.

Knowing your own **emotions** isn't just about nailing those mood swings. It's more like being your own coach—constantly reminding yourself of why you're doing what you're doing. Think about it. You've had days where you feel on top of the world, right? So when you can understand why certain things make you happy, you can recreate those conditions and stay motivated. On the flip side, if something gets you down, understanding it can steer you away from those triggers or at least prepare you for them.

And let's be honest, keeping a level head isn't just a Jedi trick. It's a **skill** you can work on. If you're aware you tend to react angrily in specific situations, practicing emotional intelligence means you catch that feeling early and manage it so that you're not doing or saying something you might regret in the heat of the moment. It also helps you avoid those mini-moments of self-sabotage that creep in from time to time.

But emotional intelligence isn't just about knowing yourself. It's about **empathy** too—your ability to step into someone else's shoes. When you're better at understanding others, it's almost like having an inside track on keeping your own emotions in check. How? Well, let's say a colleague's having a rough day and you can sense their frustration. Knowing this, you might approach work interaction differently, perhaps offering a helping hand instead of doubling down on your original plan. In turn, this keeps your environment positive and you're sticking to your disciplined approach without unnecessary static.

Having an empathetic streak might even diffuse potentially tricky situations. Got an irate customer? Instead of letting it poke your anger, being nice and finding a solution might not only save the day but keep you aligned with your disciplined, positive state.

So metaphorically speaking, emotional intelligence is like a well-maintained **garden**. Nurture and care for it, and it helps you grow stronger habits, a clearer mind, and durability during strong gusts of emotional wind. And yeah, it's one thing to know you have triggers and quite another to understand why they're there—and then tweaking your approach to life accordingly.

Through understanding your emotional triggers and having an empathetic outlook when interacting with others, you create an armor—thin, but resilient enough against the daily bumps of life. Self-discipline cements the resolve to stick to positive actions while emotional intelligence gives you the sophisticated **radar** to navigate those actions smartly.

Embrace this superpower of emotional understanding. Make it your daily **companion**, and you'll find your path to self-discipline smoother and definitely more intuitive.

The Growth Mindset Approach

So, what's the **growth mindset** all about? Simply put, it's the idea that you can get better at things and smarter just by putting in the effort and learning. Pretty comforting, right? It means you're not stuck with the hand you're dealt; you have control. It's kinda like how a gardener tends to a garden. Your **efforts** are the watering and sunlight that help things grow.

When things get tough, having this mindset really helps. Think about it. Wouldn't it be easier to push through hard times if you believed you could get better? When you face a **struggle**, if you feel it's not a dead end but a hurdle you can clear, it becomes easier to keep going. Like the old saying—"when the going gets tough, the tough get going." Believing in growth makes you that tough person.

But here's the kicker: How you talk to yourself and what you believe deeply affect your mindset. Imagine you're trying to master playing guitar. If you keep saying, "I suck at this, I'll never get it," you're not exactly setting the stage for improvement, are you? But if you tell yourself, "This is hard, but I can learn if I practice," you're building the right mindset. It's like being your own cheerleader.

Plus, your **beliefs** sneak into your thoughts and actions all the time. For instance, if you think you're not good at math, the effort you put in might reflect that belief—maybe you won't try as hard. Conversely, if you believe you can get good at math, you'll naturally seek out ways to improve, like practicing problems or asking for help.

Here's a quick story: I've always struggled with endurance running. Everything in me wanted to quit after the first mile. But, I changed the way I talked to myself. Instead of saying, "I can't keep up," I switched to, "I'm getting stronger with each run." Guess what? It worked! I got better, felt stronger, and even started to kinda like it.

Changing how you talk to yourself can be tough and feels unnatural at first. But over time, it steers you toward **growth**. Little wins along the way bolster this mindset and bit by bit, your belief system changes alongside.

Believing in your ability to grow and get smarter doesn't just keep you motivated—it reshapes your journey. When you accept that putting in effort leads to improvement, setbacks become learning opportunities instead of failures. Each **challenge** is a chance to grow stronger. It's a cycle: you believe, you act, you improve, and that reinforces your belief.

It's all interconnected. Your beliefs drive your self-talk, that fuels your actions, and your actions determine your results. Those results, in return, rebuild your beliefs. It's a whole loop of positivity.

So, consider this: Every small step or tough day isn't just something to get through. It's part of the growing process. Changing how you perceive challenges and effort reshapes your life. Transform struggles into stepping stones. Embrace the grind with a belief in growth; there is power in **persistence**.

Through this lens, success isn't about talent. And it's definitely not about luck. It's all about persistence. That growth mindset, welded into daily practice, makes falling short less scary and tries feel rewarding. Because in the end, it's not just about getting good; it's about getting better and maintaining that belief through every twist and turn.

In Conclusion

You've just dived into the **nitty-gritty** of mental toughness and how it can be your secret weapon in tackling life's curveballs. This chapter's all about giving you the lowdown on building that rock-solid foundation you need to **weather any storm**.

By getting to grips with the core components of mental toughness - control, commitment, challenge, and confidence - you're setting yourself up to be a **resilience powerhouse**. It's not just about bouncing back; it's about bouncing back stronger.

Remember, your **emotional smarts** play a huge role in keeping your cool and staying disciplined. It's all about understanding what makes you tick and managing those feelings like a pro.

And let's not forget the **game-changer** that is a growth mindset. Believing you can level up your skills with a bit of elbow grease? That's the ticket to staying **tough as nails** when the going gets rough.

This chapter's handed you a **toolbox** packed with skills to build your mental fortress. With these under your belt, you're ready to face whatever life throws your way and keep **crushing those goals**.

So, keep at it! Every challenge you tackle is another brick in your foundation of mental toughness. You've got this, and with practice, you'll be **unstoppable**. Now go out there and show the world what you're made of!

Chapter 3: Identifying and Overcoming Bad Habits

Ever found yourself stuck in a cycle of **habits** that you just can't break? It's like every time you think you've kicked that bad habit to the curb, it somehow finds its way back. But guess what — you're not alone in this **struggle**. We've all been there, wrestling with those pesky habits that seem to run our lives.

In this chapter, I'm going to share some down-to-earth ways to spot those destructive **patterns** you're dealing with. You know, the ones that sneak in and waste your time or energy every day. Then we'll chat about something called the **Habit Loop**, which kinda explains why your brain sticks to these habits like glue.

Ever heard of breaking the habit cycle? It's not just some self-help jargon. You're going to learn how to crack this **routine** and replace bad habits with good ones. And trust me, it's simpler than it sounds. I've got a straightforward **exercise** for you — habit tracking. It's like a magnifying glass for your daily routines.

Ready to **change** your life even just a little? This chapter is packed with practical tips and exercises that can spark **curiosity** about habits you've never noticed. Let's get started.

Recognizing Destructive Patterns

Destructive patterns are something we all grapple with. These are the behaviors you keep repeating, like a broken record, that mess up your progress and stop you from achieving your goals. It's like running a race with a pebble in your shoe. You need to get rid of them to move freely ahead. So, what are these habits? Simple, they're actions or thoughts that hold you back – **procrastination**, overthinking, doubting yourself, you name it.

Spotting these bad patterns isn't always a walk in the park. You've got to be really in tune with yourself, like a detective on a case. Sounds simple, right? But it involves a lot of self-reflection. Think about what **triggers** those habits. Is it stress, boredom, peer pressure, or maybe something else? Often, you might not even realize these patterns until you face a setback. Aw, crap. Did I mess up again?

Being **aware** is the cornerstone here. You won't get anywhere if you don't understand what sets these habits off. Look for common themes in the moments you messed up. Was it after a long day at work? Maybe every time you're around that one friend, you find yourself falling back into an old habit. Here's a tip: jot down notes in your phone when you see these patterns popping up. Helps connect the dots, trust me.

Now, what makes breaking these habits so hard? Mental shortcuts – that's what. Your brain loves to take the easy way out, leading you into auto-pilot. Ever found yourself opening the fridge even when you're not hungry? That's a mental shortcut. It's your brain saying, "Hey, you've done this before in this situation. Let's do it again."

These shortcuts are tricky, 'cause they've gotten you results before – even if those results aren't positive. They save you mental **energy**, which is why you keep defaulting back to them. Think of them like those comfy slippers at home. Easy to slip into, super hard to ditch when you need to put on running shoes and get moving.

It's especially tough when these habits offer some sort of instant **gratification**. Think of binge-watching shows on Netflix instead of working out. Your brain's like, "Hey, this is fun and easy, why not stick with it?" It takes a lot of effort to break this cycle where your brain is almost wired to seek the path of least resistance.

Once you're aware of these patterns and what triggers them, it gets easier to make changes. Identify what aims your brain toward that shortcut and then work on creating a new, healthier path. Slowly, as you continue to divert your thoughts and actions into better habits, those old ones start fading away. It's like rerouting a river – takes time, but the new path will eventually be just as worn as the old.

Breaking free from these patterns isn't about gigantic leaps but tiny, consistent steps. It's not a one-off job; it's a constant vigilance mix of everyday actions. You stumble, stand up, correct your course, and keep moving ahead.

Spending time to spot these destructive patterns and understanding their roots allows you down the road to build **self-discipline** and grab control of your habits. It's like turning a ship bit by bit, even tiny corrections steer you towards that destination you've been dreaming about. So go out there – reflect, spot, and tweak – your future self will definitely thank you for it.

The Habit Loop: Cue, Routine, Reward

Let's dive right into the **habit loop**. It's this pattern your brain follows to form habits. Super cool and kinda sneaky. There are three parts – the cue, routine, and reward. Think of each like pieces of a puzzle. They always fit together.

You start with the **cue**. This is like a trigger. Something that sets off a thought in your brain saying, "Hey, it's time to do that thing."

Maybe it's an emotion like feeling bored, or a situation like waking up in the morning. Boom! You're off to the races. For instance, when you wake up and see your running shoes right by the bed, that sight is the cue.

Next up is the **routine**. This is the action – what you do when that cue shows up. It's automatic. Kind of like brushing your teeth. You don't even think twice about it 'cause it's so embedded in your daily grind. Back to the running example, the sight of those shoes might drive you to lace up and head out for a jog.

Then, there's the **reward**. Super important. This is what makes you feel good after completing the routine. Maybe it's that rush of endorphins after a run or the satisfaction of ticking off an item from your to-do list. These rewards make your brain go, "Yes! Let's keep doing this." Reward ties everything together nicely, reinforcing the pattern and making sure you want to do it all over again next time.

It's pretty clear now that understanding your own habit loops is crucial. You need to get familiar with what cues you're working with and the kind of routines they trigger. Ask yourself, "What triggers got me reaching for that third donut? And what's the payoff that's keeping me in this loop?"

When you grasp your own habit loops, you're in a better place to change unwanted behaviors. You get a sort of roadmap to dissect what's going on in that noggin of yours and swap out bad habits with better ones. Let's say every afternoon you hit a slump and go for a sugary snack. What if you replace that routine? Keep the same cue – the feeling sluggish part – but change up the routine to maybe taking a quick walk outside instead? Still got a boost of energy – voila, new habit loop forming!

It's not about being perfect but knowing what's going on upstairs. Get curious. What's the trigger? What's the activity? What's the brain-reinforcing goodie at the end?

Recognize the cues swirling around your day. Maybe setting alarms or post-it notes can make you aware of them. Mess around with routines to see which ones work better. And reward yourself consciously when you pick a good habit. You start pulling these strings, you'll notice changes in your behavior easier. You got this... time to bask in the glory of breaking the bad habits by unraveling this simple trick.

Breaking the Cycle of Bad Habits

Breaking bad habits? Yeah, it ain't easy, but it's definitely worth the **effort**. You've got these unwanted behaviors that hold you back, stop you from reaching your **goals**, and just make life more complicated than it needs to be. So, figuring out how to stop those habits is crucial if you wanna change the way you act. It's like hitting the reset button.

The thing is, stopping a habit does more than just that—it reshapes your **behavior** in ways you probably haven't considered. When you quit a bad habit, you make space for something better. That's why it's so important. By ditching those unwanted habits, you break the old patterns that are holding you hostage. Those patterns? They keep you in a cycle that's hard to get out of, like running in circles and going nowhere. Stopping them is your ticket out.

Once you've got that freedom, swap bad habits for good ones to maintain the **change**. Imagine if you had a garden filled with weeds (those nasty habits). Pulling out the weeds is good but if you don't plant some lovely flowers (new habits), the weeds come back. You replace one with the other and the garden stays nice, right? Same with habits. Replacing bad juices up the motivation and keeps you from slipping back into old ways.

In my opinion, making small, manageable swaps is key here. Say you wanna stop stress-eating. After dinner, instead of heading pantry-side, you could take a walk around the block. Those tiny shifts build up into real change. A little substitute here, a tweak there and suddenly you're living a different life.

But guess what? You mess up. Keeping new habits while dealing with life's mess can torment you, making even slipping feel like some huge **failure**. And here's where I think many folks trip up—they're just too hard on themselves. Self-discipline can feel like hitting a brick wall again and again, but being kind to yourself can make all the difference. When—or rather, if—you mess up, it happens to everybody. Be patient. Your internal chatter should be more like a helpful guide than a harsh boss. Self-compassion helps slash the chance of giving up altogether.

Feeling lost? Here's a trick: don't view setbacks as end-all failures. If you could see setbacks as part of the learning curve, things could shift in your favor. When you stumble—and we all do—give yourself a moment to breathe, check out why you fell, and plan a gentle way back onto the path. I mean, who's ever learned to ride a bike without some bruises?

And how about celebrating your **progress**? Not just the big ones but even the small victories. Managed to swap your evening snack routine once? Great! Did the walk instead of couch-slouch? Awesome! Celebrate. Let these little wins pile up, motivating you and giving you enough **confidence** to keep at it.

So, stopping bad habits, swapping them for good ones, and leaning into self-kindness is your trifecta for successful **change**. Things'll go off the rails now and then, but every new morning brings the chance to reset and try again. Keep at it—you're not just breaking habits, you're changing your life.

Replacing Negative Behaviors with Positive Ones

You want to **ditch** those bad habits and replace them with good ones? Smart move. Getting rid of stuff you don't want to do is tough, but swapping it with things you care about makes it way easier. Picture this: Every bad habit you ditch leaves an empty spot. If you don't fill it with a good habit, the bad one sneaks back in.

Think about it. If you're trying to quit smoking, you can't leave your hands and mouth empty. You could start chewing gum or taking more walks, maybe start knitting if you're into that. The idea is to give your **brain** something better to focus on. Seems simple, right? But, here's the trick – you have to choose new habits that really match up with what you care about and your big-picture goals.

It's like this: If your goal is to get fit, replacing binge-watching TV with going for a run is a solid swap. Not only does running fill the time, but it also pushes you closer to your fitness goals. But if your heart's not into running, maybe dancing or swimming works better for you. The point is, the new **habit** should resonate with what you really care about. Otherwise, it won't stick.

Now, let's talk about your **environment**. Setting up your surroundings can make a giant difference. Imagine you're trying to eat healthier but your kitchen's full of chips and cookies... yikes! You're just setting yourself up for failure. Swap out the junk food with fruits, nuts, and healthy snacks. Keep them at eye level where you can easily grab 'em. Make your environment work with you, not against you.

Here's another tip: If you're wanting to write more, set up a cozy writing nook. Have your computer, journals, pens – all that good stuff ready. Maybe toss a comfy chair in there. Make it a place that's inviting and gets you in the mood to write. That way, you're more likely to stick with it.

And don't forget the **people** around you. Navigating environments can extend to your friendships. If your buddies are constant binge-watchers and snackers, it's going to be even harder to stick to new, healthy habits. Maybe find a new crowd that loves doing what you want to do – join a book club, running group, or cooking class. Aligning your social circle with your new habits can be a game-changer.

Here's a fun trick your brain will appreciate: link new habits to **routines** you already have. Want to do more reading each night? Tack it onto brushing your teeth. When you see your toothbrush, grab your book, too. This way, the old habit reinforces the new one.

So, to sum it all up: Ditch bad habits by grabbing hold of good ones that you care about and that fit into your **goals**. Surround yourself with an environment that pushes you towards success and make sure your friends are cool with supporting your new lifestyle. Stick your new habits to routines you already got going, and you'll be golden. You'll feel better in no time.

Practical Exercise: Habit Tracking and Analysis

Hey there! Let's dive into a super useful exercise for tackling those **bad habits** you want to shake. Here's how you can get started:

First, **pick** one bad habit you want to change. It's gotta be something that really bugs you—think of stuff like eating junk food late at night, biting your nails, or even checking your phone every other minute. Just focus on one for now.

Once you've nailed it down, grab a notebook. **Write** down when, where, and how you feel each time you do this habit. Do it for a week. Make a little note every single time. For example, "Tuesday, 2 PM, on couch, bored" or "Friday, 8 PM, in bed, stressed out."

After your week of **tracking** is done, it's time to play detective. Look at your notes and see if you can spot any patterns. Is it always happening in the afternoon? Maybe it's the same place every time? What about your mood—are you tired, angry, or just plain bored?

Here's where things get interesting. **Think** about what need or reward this habit is giving you. Maybe that late-night snack is comforting, or checking your phone makes you feel connected. These rewards are why the habit sticks around.

Now, switch gears. Come up with some better **alternatives** that can give you the same benefit without the downside. If you're snacking late at night for comfort, maybe drinking herbal tea could help. For nail-biting, try squeezing a stress ball instead.

Once you've got some alternatives in mind, it's time to make a **plan**. Decide when and how you're going to start doing this new behavior. Write it down. Maybe even put reminders on your phone or sticky notes in places you'll see them.

And now comes the part where you stick with it. Keep **track** of how you're doing—just like you did with the original habit. Write down your successes and struggles. You'll find this really helps you see progress. You might need to tweak things here or there over the next month. That's totally normal, and part of the process.

By breaking it down like this, you're making what feels like a massive change into bite-sized pieces (pun intended if you picked late-night snacking!).

You've probably noticed that the essence of this exercise is understanding yourself better. It's like holding up a mirror to see what's really going on, rather than just the habit itself. This deeper understanding is what'll help you come up with truly effective alternatives.

Here's a little tip—don't get disheartened if you don't succeed immediately. Think of it like learning to ride a bike. You might wobble a bit initially but keep at it. Your old habits took years to form, so it's okay if new, better ones take a little time too.

So there you have it—a practical way to kick that bad habit to the curb and introduce a positive one instead. Why not give it a shot and see how it goes? Let's chat next time about refining those strategies and keeping the good vibes flowing. You're doing awesome!

In Conclusion

This chapter offers **valuable** insights and strategies to help you identify and overcome bad habits. By understanding the habits that hold you back and learning effective techniques to break them, you can make **positive** changes in your life.

You've seen what destructive patterns are and how they affect your personal **growth**. You've learned about the importance of knowing your habit loops: cue, routine, reward. You've discovered how to break the **cycle** of bad habits and replace them with positive actions. You've explored the role of self-awareness and self-compassion in overcoming setbacks. And you've seen how habit **tracking** and analysis can help you make lasting changes.

With these tools at your disposal, it's time to take a proactive step towards becoming the best version of yourself. Small changes in **behavior** can lead to big improvements in your life. Stay committed, be patient, and remember that every effort counts. With **determination**, you'll master your habits and reach your **goals**!

I'm confident that you can make these changes. It's not always easy, but it's definitely worth it. Keep pushing forward, and don't be too hard on yourself if you slip up now and then. Rome wasn't built in a day, and neither are new habits. You've got this!

Chapter 4: Resisting Temptations Effectively

Ever wondered why it's so tough to resist reaching for that extra slice of pizza or endlessly scrolling through your phone? **Temptations** sneak up on all of us.

When I think about **success** and personal control, it boils down to just one thing—mastering the art of resisting temptations. It might sound tricky, right? But stick with me here because what you'll find in this chapter will change how you handle those pesky impulses.

You've got that **drive**, that urge to be better, but sometimes it's like you're wrestling with unseen forces. In this chapter, we pull back the curtain on what makes temptations so, well, tempting. You'll learn about quirky **tricks** and simple hacks to tighten up your impulse control. Imagine finding ways to say "no" to those instant gratifications that tug at you daily.

Think about setting up your **space** to better fight off those urges. Pretty cool, huh? It's like setting traps for your temptations. Plus, you'll get a practical **exercise** where you can see how well you manage facing off with these sneaky intruders and come out on top.

Ready to get the upper hand on your daily **battles** and make life a bit smoother? Dive right in—you'll love what's coming. This chapter is all about giving you the **tools** to resist temptations effectively and take control of your life.

Understanding the Nature of Temptations

You're strolling down the street, laser-focused on your **task**, when suddenly, the aroma of freshly baked doughnuts hits you. That mouth-watering smell triggers something powerful in your **brain**. So, what's really going on in your head right now?

When you're faced with these situations—like that tempting smell—your mind kicks into high gear. See, your brain's got this knack for finding shortcuts. When it processes those seductive scents, your reward system goes off like a **fire alarm**. You feel a pull, a craving. That's your limbic system talking, the part of your brain that's all about pleasure and survival. Sounds pretty basic, right? Well, it's these gut reactions that are often the trickiest to keep in check.

Now, let's talk **dopamine**. This chemical messenger is usually the culprit. When you're faced with a tempting treat, it's dopamine that lights up your brain, screaming, "Yes! This will make you happy!" But dopamine doesn't just egg you on. It's like your brain's personal historian, stockpiling that info for future reference. So, the next time you catch a whiff of doughnuts, there's already a little voice in your head reminding you how good they were last time. Sneaky, huh?

Dopamine's a tricky playmate. Not only does it lure you into **temptation** by highlighting the immediate pleasure, but it also etches that experience into your memory. That's why you tend to fall for the same traps over and over. Breaking that dopamine chain isn't a walk in the park. But knowing how it works gives you a fighting chance.

With the stage set, your real challenge lies in spotting your own **triggers**. Because let's face it, knowing the theory isn't enough—you've got to catch yourself in action. So, how do you do it? Start by noticing patterns. Do you reach for snacks whenever you binge-watch TV? Does stress send you straight to online shopping? The idea here is to zero in on when and where these triggers pop up.

Mapping out these patterns helps, big time. Keep a small **journal** handy to note when you feel a pull toward a bad habit. You'd be surprised how much self-truth you uncover by simply jotting down thoughts. This awareness won't just help you understand your weak spots. It also builds a strategy for tackling them head-on.

Catching and acknowledging temptation triggers is half the **battle**. Sure, it's tedious, but let's be honest, winning against these strong impulses feels pretty darn rewarding. Once you spot your patterns, you gain control, making it easier to resist the urges that sidetrack your goals.

In a nutshell, understanding temptations is like being in a constant chess game with your brain. Recognize its moves—like the dopamine play or those sneaky triggers. Spot the usual suspects in your day-to-day routines. By doing this, you set the stage for overcoming **distractions** like a pro.

Strategies for Impulse Control

We've all been there. That moment when your **brain** pushes you to eat that extra slice of cake or buy something you really don't need. Impulses, right? They can get the better of you if you're not careful. Let's chat about how to get a grip on these pesky urges with some practical strategies.

One useful method for managing impulsive **actions** involves having a plan in place, something called an "if-then" plan. It's like having a script ready for situations where you know you might fall into your usual habits. Simple idea- If x happens, then you'll do y. For example, "If I feel like ordering takeout, then I'll drink a glass of water first and wait 20 minutes." This pre-planned decision helps cut off the **impulse** before it takes over. It's all about redirecting your mind away from the immediate action it craves.

To see how this works, imagine you're walking by your favorite bakery. The smell of fresh cookies hits you, and you're about to walk in and buy one (or six). But you've got your "if-then" plan. You've decided, "If I crave sweets, then I'll chew gum instead." Might sound way too simple, but it's all about creating a new pattern for your brain to follow. It needs to become your go-to reaction.

Another important part of controlling impulses is being **self-aware**. If you can catch those urges early, you've got a much better chance of stopping them. Sounds easy, right? Not always. You need to keep checking in with yourself throughout the day. Start by noticing how you feel right before the urge hits. Are you stressed? Bored? Frustrated? Pinpointing these emotional triggers helps you see the pattern.

Think about keeping a little **journal**. Each time you feel an impulse, jot down what you're feeling. Over time, you'll start seeing trends. Maybe you always want something sweet when you're stressed at work or feel like spending money right after watching a favorite TV show. Awareness really is the first step to change. Once you're aware, you can put strategies in place ahead of time, just like with those "if-then" plans.

Now, let's dive into another tool—the "urge surfing" method. This works by riding out the urge like you'd surf a wave. When an urge comes, instead of giving in immediately, you pay attention to it. But you don't act on it. The key here is to notice how the urge feels in your body. It might start strong, but urges are usually temporary. They swell up like a wave and eventually crash down.

Here's how you could try it: let's say you feel tempted to scroll through social media during work. Stop and notice that urge. Where do you feel it? In your hands, itching to grab your phone? In your mind, creating an impatient buzz? Close your eyes. Really feel it.

You'll notice that after a few minutes, it starts to fade. That's the wave crashing.

Riding the urge wave can give you a sense of **control** and **confidence**. You're not ignoring the urge, so it doesn't feel like you're depriving yourself. And you definitely don't feel like you're fighting a losing battle. It's just about accepting that it's there and waiting for it to pass.

All these techniques—if-then plans, self-awareness, and urge surfing—come together to create a solid toolkit for dealing with impulsive actions. It's normal to falter now and then. Don't beat yourself up about those moments. What matters is that you're trying, that you're aware, and you're equipped with ways to handle those urges effectively. So next time those **temptations** strike, you'll be ready to handle them like a pro.

Delayed Gratification Techniques

Ever noticed how easily thinking short-term can mess up your plans? You see, if you're always **focused** on what feels good right now, you might end up making choices that aren't so great in the long run. Like, skipping the gym to binge-watch a new show or splurging on stuff you don't really need. It's about those little choices that pile up, pushing you away from your **goals**.

Now, short-term thinking. It's like being stuck in the moment, where the latest, flashiest thing catches your eye. You get a small rush from it, which makes it super tempting to dive right in—ignoring what actually might be better for you later. But that quick hit of pleasure? It can trick your brain into thinking it's a great deal, while your bigger goals end up taking a backseat.

But what if you took those quick rewards and zoomed out a bit? Think of them like tiny puzzle pieces. Sure, a single piece might look cool on its own, but when you see it as part of the full picture—a complete puzzle of your long-term vision—it gets a lot more meaningful. So, those quick perks aren't bad in themselves. They just need to fit into the broader tapestry. See a small win, but make sure it's part of guiding you toward that final **goal**.

Now, let's talk about picturing your future self. That's a nifty trick to help in holding off on immediate rewards for something better. Close your eyes, and **imagine** who you wanna be five years down the line. It's like having a chat with future-you. Ask, "Would they care if I skipped this workout, or bought this shiny thing?" Nine times out of ten, future-you will grin and say, "Nah. I'm more into the endgame."

Seriously, take a minute every day to do this. Whether you're standing in line debating that second latte or contemplating another snooze button hit, future-you can be a real guide. They can steer you away from traps and right into what really matters.

Think about those marathon runners **training** for months. They probably wanted to quit or eat junk food plenty of times. But it's their future self—crossing that finish line—that kept 'em going. If they can delay **gratification** for months, you can hold off a little longer for what truly counts too.

Transitioning out of the here-and-now mindset can be kind of liberating. Once you start seeing things from this angle, it's like having a new pair of glasses. **Decisions** seem clearer, less clouded by the immediate and more geared towards the ultimate goal you're chasing. So next time you're at a crossroads between instant fun and long-term gain, whip out that mental image of a high-fiving future-you. Feels good, right?

To wrap things up, remember it's about shifting your lens. Moving from the immediate to the bigger picture, leaning on future-you for wisdom, and seeing quick rewards as just pieces of something larger. These **techniques** won't just enhance your self-discipline;

they'll make the path ahead a lot more satisfying. So, go on, give your future self a pat on the back... they're waiting for you.

Environmental Design for Temptation Resistance

Let's kick things off with the idea of **choice architecture**. It's like setting up your own environment in a way that makes the good stuff easy to reach and the bad stuff hard to get to. Picture yourself setting a trap—but in a nice way. This tactic helps keep you from falling prey to those pesky temptations.

To make this work, you've got to really think about your **physical spaces**. If the candy bowl's within arm's reach, you'll probably dip your hand in more times than you'd like to admit. But stick it on the top shelf where you'd need a ladder to reach it, and suddenly, your snacking impulse shrinks. The same goes for your workspace: got distractions? Move 'em out of sight. Lower the clutter, and you'll boost your focus.

In your **digital space**, it's much the same story. How often do you start doing something productive only to end up scrolling through social media for ages? Setting up website blockers or screen time limits can work wonders. If you tuck those tempting apps in a hidden folder or even wipe them from your phone's home screen, you'll cut down on those mindless taps.

Here's a little secret: "Out of sight, out of mind" isn't just a saying—it's the truth. If whatever tempts you isn't in your face all the time, it's easier to forget it's even there. If chocolate's your downfall, don't stash it in your desk drawer. Store it in the fridge or better yet, don't buy it at all. But this rule doesn't just apply to junk food. Got a project you're trying to finish but your phone keeps buzzing? Chuck it in another room. Seriously, lock it away. You'll find yourself getting more done.

Tidying up your space can also make a big difference. Think of your neat desk like a clean canvas. It's inviting, right? A cluttered desk? Feels overwhelming. An organized space fosters clear thinking and makes slipping into bad habits less likely. I've found a nicely set-up workspace makes me want to sit and knock out tasks.

And it's not just about putting stuff out of sight; it's also about adding positive **triggers** in your environment. Want to remember your goal? Maybe place inspiration near your workspace—a sticky note with a motivational quote or a picture of something you're working towards. These visual cues can keep you grounded.

When it comes to working out, place your **exercise gear** where you see it first thing in the morning. Gym stuff on your bedroom chair? You're more likely to actually use it. It's kind of like giving yourself a gentle nudge.

With digital spaces, the same rules apply. Use **productivity tools** like Trello or Asana but keep them simple and uncluttered. Pop-ups that push you about daunting tasks will only stress you out. Make them user-friendly and to the point.

So, here's the gist: tweak your environment. Remove the bad stuff, bring in the good. Sometimes, tiny changes in how you set things up can make a real dent in your temptations and make sticking to your goals way easier. Now go ahead, try rearranging your world with these ideas. You might be surprised how much they help!

Practical Exercise: Temptation Exposure and Response Prevention

Let's talk about facing your **temptations** head-on. Sounds daring, right? Don't worry; we're gonna break it down step by step.

First, pick one specific temptation you want to tackle. It could be anything: snacking late at night, endlessly scrolling through social media, or skipping workouts. Got one in mind? Great.

Now, set up a controlled **environment** where you can face this temptation without completely giving in. This means you should create a safe space where you're near the temptation, but not all the way immersed. It's like dipping your toes in the water instead of diving headfirst. Let's say it's that bowl of chips you can't resist at 10 PM. Place it in sight at your kitchen table, but you're not allowed to touch it just yet.

So, you're facing the temptation. Here comes the tricky part – watching your thoughts and physical sensations mindfully. This means pay attention to what's happening in your body and mind. Feeling your mouth water? Heart racing a bit? What thoughts are popping up? Just notice, don't act. This is your chance to observe without judgment. Essentially, you become a kind of detective, gathering clues about your **triggers**.

When those urges to give in get strong, maybe even relentless, try using deep **breathing** or distraction. Deep breathing helps. Take a few deep breaths in through your nose and out through your mouth. Feel it calm your racing heart. Still can't resist? Distract yourself. Start a conversation, read a few pages of a book, or count backward from 100. Anything to take the edge off those cravings.

As you get the hang of resisting over short bursts of time, start extending your exposure gradually. If you faced that bowl of chips for five minutes today, next time push it to ten. So, eventually, you sit confidently next to it without even flinching. Building **stamina**, bit by bit. Think of it like lifting slightly heavier weights each gym session.

After each session, jot down your experience. What exactly happened when you saw and resisted the temptation? Did the deep breathing work, or was the distraction more effective? Also note any patterns you observe. Maybe cravings spike when you're frustrated or bored. Really, anything that sheds a little light on your struggle.

Thinking about your **progress** is vital. Over time, you'll see improvements. Maybe you're now able to resist snacking for longer, or perhaps those social media urges are way easier to manage. If you notice a stalling point, tweak your approach. Maybe try a different distraction or tweak that controlled environment slightly to up the challenge.

Piece by piece, you're building a **strategy** that works. One brick at a time, you're constructing your wall of resistance against those temptations. Feels good, doesn't it? Keep pushing, keep tweaking, and watch yourself grow stronger in ways you probably didn't think were possible.

There you go. Bit by bit, facing temptation doesn't seem quite as daunting. With each step, you're closer to crushing those bad habits and staying true to achieving your **goals**. Keep it up – you're on the right track.

Conclusion

In this chapter, we've explored **essential strategies** for resisting temptations. Understanding the underlying mechanisms and developing practical techniques can **empower** you to maintain self-discipline and achieve your goals more effectively.

You've learned about how temptations work in our **brains** and how dopamine makes them stronger. We've covered techniques to **identify** when and why you feel tempted, and how "urge surfing" helps in managing strong desires. You've also seen how changing your **environment** can reduce temptations.

These **key strategies** from this chapter will help you resist temptations, stay **focused**, and reach your ambitions. With practice and persistence, you're well on your way to **mastering** self-discipline!

Remember, it's all about understanding your triggers and developing the tools to overcome them. By applying what you've learned, you'll find yourself better equipped to handle those tricky situations that used to trip you up. It's not about being perfect, but about making progress one step at a time.

So, go ahead and put these techniques into action. You might be surprised at how much easier it becomes to stick to your goals when you've got these strategies up your sleeve. Keep at it, and before you know it, you'll be crushing those temptations like a pro!

Chapter 5: Goal Setting and Achievement

Ever felt like you're running in circles, always **busy** but never quite getting where you want to go? Well, you're not alone. This chapter's about to shake things up. You'll find yourself looking at your **goals** in a whole new way. Intrigued? You should be.

You probably know that having goals is crucial, but **setting** them right and then actually reaching them—that's where the real magic happens. In this chapter, you're going to learn how to set goals that truly **matter** to you. No more shooting blindly in the dark. This is where you make it count.

So why should you care? Because mastering this skill can literally change how you **approach** everything in life. Imagine slicing those big dreams into little, doable steps. And yeah, we're going to talk about the **obstacles** too—let's face it, everyone hits roadblocks. You'll discover how to deal with those bumps in the road.

Up for a challenge? Great. You'll get a practical **exercise** that'll help you map out your goals. Think of it as your personal roadmap. By the end of this chapter, you won't just be reading about goals—you'll be **crushing** them.

Ready to dive in? Let's get the ball rolling.

SMART Goal Framework

Setting **goals** isn't just about jotting down thoughts and wishes you have for the future. It's about giving those dreams a shape, and being **specific** is crucial in this process. Why? Well, if you're not clear about what you want, it's way too easy to lose steam. Imagine saying, "I want to be healthier..." It's vague, right? It doesn't give you a road map. But say, "I want to lose 10 pounds in three months..." Suddenly, the path seems a bit clearer. You know where you're headed, and that's a huge boost for **motivation**.

Let's say you want to run a 5K race. If your plan is just "run more," it's easy to cheat yourself out of the effort. But if you spell it out—"run three times a week for 30 minutes"—you've painted a picture. Each run becomes a step in your journey.

Next up is making sure your goals can be **measured**. If you can't track them, how will you know you're knocking it out of the park—or falling behind? Measurement isn't just a way to keep tabs on progress; it's your personal cheerleading squad. When you see how much you've improved, you're more likely to keep going. So, instead of saying "get better grades," try "raise my GPA by 0.2 points this semester." Or if it's about fitness, "run a mile in under eight minutes." Specific and measurable goals make it easier to stay pumped up and on track.

OK, you've got your measurable goal. Now, it's time to talk about **backward planning**. This is where you make things doable. Imagine you're making a delicious sandwich. You don't just slap stuff on bread and hope it's tasty. Nope. You think about each layer. The same goes for setting goals. Start at the finish line—what do you want to achieve? Let's say you're aiming to buy a car in a year. Think backward from that goal. How much money will you need to save? Break it down monthly, weekly, even daily if it helps.

By using this method, you're slicing your big goal into smaller, bite-sized pieces. This doesn't just help in organization; it reduces overwhelm. This way, when you've saved that little bit of money each week, it doesn't feel like a herculean task by the end.

Don't forget about **deadlines**. They're like little magic tricks. Without a deadline, you might end up wandering. Commit to a timeline and it somehow finds a way to push you forward. Let's say you want to learn a new skill, something like, oh, playing the guitar. Instead of just saying you'll practice, carve out a timeframe. "I'll learn three new songs in two months." There you go – you have a target to hit.

But here's a twist. While it's great to give your goals a timeline, be kind to yourself in setting it. Goals should be **challenging** yet **realistic**. If they're too tough, it's easy to throw in the towel. Too easy, and you might get bored. Try balancing it out, kind of like walking a tightrope.

So, there you have it: the ingredients for the SMART Goal sandwich. Be specific to spur your motivation. Measure it to see your progress. Use backward planning to keep it feasible. Put everything on a timeline to stick to the route. Not so complicated when broken down, right?

Aligning Goals with Personal Values

Setting **goals** is great, but setting goals based on your personal **values**? That's a total game changer. Imagine every target you set being something you're genuinely passionate about. Feels pretty powerful, right? It amps up your inner **drive** like nothing else. Here's the thing: when your goals align with what you truly value, **motivation** doesn't feel forced. It's something that comes naturally.

First, you need to understand your personal values to see what really matters to you. This part sounds a bit intense, but trust me, it's like cleaning out your closet — super satisfying once you get into it.

Grab a piece of paper or your phone and jot down things you genuinely care about. Family? Success at work? Adventure? Helping others? Write it all down. Once you've got your list, rank them in order of importance. This helps you see at a glance what your top values are. Take some time to think about why these values are important. Sometimes the 'why' makes things even clearer.

Alright, you've got your values sorted out. Next is how you match them to your goals. This is where the values-goals **alignment** matrix comes in. Don't worry, it sounds way more complicated than it is.

Set up a simple matrix. One axis is for your values, the other for your goals. List your values along one side. They act like anchors. Write your goals along the other side.

Now, start pairing your goals with your values. For each goal, ask yourself a couple things:

- Does this goal uphold any of my values?

- How does achieving this goal support what I care most about?

Circle those goals that really sync up with your values. Those are your sweet spots, where your **motivation** is going to be sky-high.

Let's take an example. Say one of your values is family, and a goal you have is to advance in your job. You might think, "How does becoming a manager help my family?" Maybe it's a better salary that provides more stability at home. Boom—alignment. Or, if your value is adventure, and your goal is to run a marathon, that's probably a no-brainer.

But what if your goal doesn't fit in with any of your values? Well, it might not be the right goal for you. It's harsh but hey, sometimes it's good to reassess what you think you want.

To wrap things up:

- Write down what values matter most to you.

- Set goals that align with those values using that matrix.

- Make adjustments if necessary.

You'll soon see that when your goals line up with your values, achieving them doesn't feel like a chore. Instead, it just feels right. It's almost like having a natural, unspoken **contract** with yourself.

So, go ahead. Look deep, figure out what truly **fuels** you, and steer your goals in that direction. It'll help you not just achieve them but live them authentically.

Breaking Down Long-Term Goals into Actionable Steps

Ever feel like a big project is this giant, scary thing you don't even know where to start with? Well, that's pretty normal. But don't sweat it, I've got some simple tips to help you out. We'll chat about **goal** layers, how to whip up a goal chart, and the 90-day sprint trick to keep you on track.

Goal Layers

Think of your overall **goal** as a cake. Yep, a cake has layers. Some are thin, some are thick, but they all stack up to make something awesome. It's the same with big goals. Breaking 'em down into smaller chunks makes them way easier to handle.

Take something huge like "launching your own **business**." Feels overwhelming if you don't look at the layers. Your top layer's the main idea - starting your business. Here's what sits beneath:

- Research the market

- Create a business plan

- Seek funding

- Develop a product

- Market your product

Each of these steps is a goal layer that you can tackle bit by bit. It all helps in taming the chaos and making the seemingly impossible totally doable.

Goal Breakdown Chart

Alright, how do you get this all on paper and spot the key steps? Easy peasy. Create a goal chart. Grab a piece of paper or an app or whatever floats your boat. Jot down your big **goal** at the top, like the title of our cake. Under that, list your main chunks (those layers we yakked about).

For "Research the market," write smaller tasks:

- Read articles on industry trends

- Survey potential customers

- Analyze competitors

For "Create a business plan":

- Outline your business structure

- Fill in financial projections

- Plan your marketing strategy

Each chunk or layer should be made up of specific tasks. This way, you're seeing each part, step-by-step, making the entire project way less scary. It's amazing how breaking it down can make a huge difference.

90-Day Sprint Method

Picture this: you've got a long-distance marathon. Terrifying, right? What if instead of the long slog, you had shorter races leading into each other? That's your sprinting technique for conquering long-term goals. Enter the 90-day **sprint**. It keeps you pumped without feeling like you're gonna keel over.

How does it work? Break down your big goal and its layers into 90-day chunks. Simple steps:

- Set clear objectives for each sprint

- Choose what to nail in those 3 months

- List daily or weekly tasks

Let's say your goal is taking three months to develop your **product**. Tackle one step: Prototyping the product. Here's where a structured to-do list comes in handy. Listing steps:

- Week 1-2: Design sketches

- Week 3-4: Create prototypes

- Week 5-6: User testing

- Week 7-8: Adjust based on feedback

- Week 9-10: Prep for production

By making a solid game plan for each sprint, things look a whole lot more achievable at the end. Small bites, don't choke on 'em!

Keeping the Momentum

There's another piece to this puzzle. Staying fired up. How often do we start with guns blazing and then fizzle out? A lot. But keeping sprints can curb this. Always review what's done and what's coming up.

Have visual reminders - sticky notes, alarm alerts. Anything that keeps your **goal** front and center. Rewards after each sprint help too... like treating yourself for keeping up. It's about maintaining a steady pace without burning out.

Mixing goal layers with detailed charts and productive sprints can totally transform how long-term goals feel. It's worth giving it a shot, aligning your daily tasks towards that seemingly monstrous **project**. Easier said than done? Practice it bit by bit, and you'll find it's totally doable.

Make those **dreams** a tangible reality, step by step!

Overcoming Obstacles in Goal Pursuit

You've set some **goals** and you're pumped to go after them. Awesome! But have you thought about what could trip you up? Thinking about those roadblocks ahead of time is crucial. Why? Imagine starting a road trip without checking the weather or road conditions. Not so smart, right? The same goes for goal setting. If you're aware of possible setbacks, you're better equipped to dodge 'em.

Think about it. Nothing kills **motivation** faster than getting blindsided. Maybe your goal is to hit the gym every morning. But what if your alarm doesn't go off one day? Or maybe you're aiming to write a novel, but then life throws a wrench in your plans with unexpected errands. Having some backup plans can help you stay on track instead of spiraling out.

So, how do you prep for these hiccups? Start by brainstorming common issues. For instance:

• Plan A: Workout in the morning.

Backup Plan: Evening workout if mornings fail.

• Plan A: Write 500 words daily.

Backup Plan: Write 1,000 words on weekends to catch up.

See? It's like having a safety net. If one plan falls through, another picks up the slack. It helps keep things moving forward.

Let's dig a little deeper into a super cool technique for this: "if-then **planning**." Sound complicated? It's not. Think of it like coding yourself to act in specific situations. You set up little mental flags – if situations happen, then responses kick in automatically.

For example:

• If the alarm doesn't ring, then I'll go to an evening class.

• If I miss my word count, then I'll set aside extra time over the weekend to write.

This kind of if-then thing works wonders because you're preemptively handling potential screw-ups. It's like setting up a series of dominoes where tipping over the first triggers a necessary action to stay on course.

Not only does this keep you prepared, but it also reduces **stress**. You're giving yourself permission to not be perfect. Unexpected stuff happens – that's life. What matters is how swiftly you respond and adapt, without beating yourself up.

Let's say your goal is to stick to a healthy **diet**, but you often get thrown off by surprise lunch meetings. Simple. If there's an unexpected lunch meeting, then you'll choose the healthiest option available. That's it. No fuss.

Adaptability is key. Think about sailors – they can't control the wind but can adjust their sails. By prepping your if-then plans, you're doing the same. Instead of getting bogged down by disruptions, you adjust course and keep sailing toward your goals.

Here's another point: don't go overboard. Too many plans can overwhelm you. Focus on the main **hurdles** you're likely to face first. Keep it simple to begin, you're more likely to stick to it.

So next time you've got a new goal in mind, don't just think about how cool the end result will be. Think through what's gonna get in your way, make backup plans, and employ the if-then planning method. That way, you'll stay **resilient** and keep pushing forward, no matter what **obstacles** pop up.

Practical Exercise: Creating a Personal Goal Roadmap

Think about that big **long-term goal** you've been itching to reach. Maybe it's running a marathon, launching your own business, or mastering a new language. It's easy to feel overwhelmed by what seems like a monster of a task. But if you narrow it down, hitting that finish line won't seem so daunting.

The trick here is chopping that huge **goal** into smaller, more manageable steps. Break it up like you would a complicated recipe. Don't worry about the whole dish just yet; focus on mixing the batter first. Smaller steps feel less overwhelming, and each one builds a bit of momentum. That's when you'll feel like you're getting somewhere.

Next, work out a **timeline**—think about it in reverse order. Start from your end goal and map your way back to the present. It's like finding your way out of a maze. Knowing your end goal helps you pinpoint key milestones along the way and gives you an idea of how long each will take. And let's be real, having a timeline is a huge motivation booster. Deadlines turn daydreams into to-do lists.

But we all know, the road to any goal isn't exactly smooth. You're bound to hit a bump or two. Try to anticipate a few of these and prepare **backup plans**. If you're aiming for that marathon, maybe you'll face a few rainy days where running outside isn't an option. Have some indoor exercises lined up. Planning for roadblocks means fewer surprises, and fewer surprises mean less stress.

Now, what **actions** will get you to each small step? Be specific here. For example, if your goal is a business, you might need tasks like market research, starting your website, and drafting a business plan. Listing out what you need to do keeps your path clear and helps you focus on what's next without feeling all over the place.

Each small action item needs its own **deadline** too. Yes, more deadlines! They aren't just for big goals. If you set friendly little due dates for your steps, it'll keep you moving steadily. Keep these timelines realistic to avoid the threat of burnout.

No roadmap is complete without a visual. Make a **map** of your goal—it could be a chart, a vision board, or an app like Trello. Think of this as your mission control board, something you'll look at often to remind yourself where you're heading and what's next in line.

Lastly, plan regular **check-ins**. This is crucial. Every week or month, sit down, see where you are, what's working, and what isn't. Tiny tweaks here and there keep your course corrections manageable. If those big chunks seem too much, that's your opportunity to divide them again.

A journey of a thousand miles starts with a single step—so start stepping!

Conclusion

You've gained **valuable insights** about setting and achieving goals in a way that aligns with your personal values and maintains focus on long-term objectives. By breaking down **complexities** and anticipating potential setbacks, you can pave a clearer path to your dreams. This understanding will ultimately **empower** you to not only set goals but follow through with them efficiently and effectively.

Throughout this chapter, you've learned:

• The importance of setting specific and clear goals to boost **motivation**

• How tracking progress with measurable goals keeps **momentum** going

• How ease of goal completion increases with backward planning

• Aligning personal values with goals for intrinsic motivation

• Deeper preparedness by planning for potential obstacles

These takeaways could bring big changes to the way you go after your goals. With these **strategies** in mind, it's time for you to put them to work and transform your **aspirations** into reality. Keep these lessons close, be proactive, and stay determined. Always moving forward, you've got the tools now to achieve your goals. Stay **inspired**!

Chapter 6: Time Management for Self-Discipline

Ever wished you had more hours in the day? Yeah, me too. As I sat at my desk one late night, surrounded by a forest of sticky notes and half-empty coffee cups, I realized something had to change. **Time** was slipping through my fingers, and it felt like I'd never get ahead.

Imagine having the power to **structure** your day so well that you actually get things done. Sounds good, right? Well, that's what this chapter is all about. It's not just about ticking off tasks but making real **progress**.

So, let's get to the heart of it. You'll learn ways to figure out what's really **important** and what can wait. You'll see how short bursts of **focus**, like sprinting but for your brain, can get you miles ahead. And guess what? You'll also cut out all those bad habits that steal your time.

Picture this: at the end of this chapter, you'll not only know how to make a to-do list, but make it **work** for you. Plus, there's a little **exercise** at the end to shape up your schedule. Bet you're curious already, huh? Well, let's just say you're closer than ever to **mastering** your time. Why wouldn't you want to?

You're about to dive into some game-changing strategies that'll help you take control of your day. From prioritizing tasks to eliminating time-wasters, you'll learn how to squeeze the most out of every hour. And the best part? These aren't just boring tips—they're practical, easy-to-implement techniques that'll have you wondering how you ever managed without them.

So, are you ready to kiss goodbye to those late nights and frantic rushes to meet deadlines? Great! Let's jump right in and start turning your time management dreams into reality.

Prioritization Techniques

Knowing the difference between **urgent** and **important** tasks is super crucial for time management and self-discipline. When you focus only on urgent stuff, you're basically just putting out fires all day. It feels like you're busy, but you often end up neglecting the important things that could really move the needle. Think about that big project you have for work—it might not be due tomorrow, but if you keep setting it aside for urgent emails, you'll eventually hit a wall.

Alright, so to help make sense of it all, let's talk about the **Eisenhower Matrix**. It's named after Dwight D. Eisenhower, but you don't need to remember that—what's important is how it helps you. It's like four boxes: Urgent and Important, Important but Not Urgent, Urgent but Not Important, and Neither Urgent nor Important.

Here's how to use it:

• Urgent and Important: These are the tasks you should tackle right away. They usually have deadlines and serious consequences if not done. Stuff like last-minute projects or pressing problems.

• Important but Not Urgent: These tasks are key for long-term goals. They won't scream for your attention, but focusing on them can change your life. Think about reading a new book to gain skills or starting a fitness regime.

- Urgent but Not Important: These tasks can be tricky because they demand attention but don't contribute much to your long-term goals. Answering that phone call or responding to low-priority emails falls here. Maybe delegate these if you can.

- Neither Urgent nor Important: Honestly, these tasks are just distractions. Browsing social media or watching random videos online. This box is a pitfall for procrastination. Just, avoid.

Now, let's switch gears to the **ABC method** for ranking tasks. It's another way to sort through what's important, but in a more straightforward ranking system.

- A tasks: Must-dos. High-priority and with major consequences if they're not done. Think completing a critical work assignment.

- B tasks: Should-dos. They're important, but the sky won't fall if they're not done today. Like following up on an email or making that dentist appointment.

- C tasks: Nice-to-dos. They're more like filler tasks. You'd like to do them, but there aren't any serious consequences if they don't happen soon. For instance, organizing your workspace or sorting photos on your phone.

With the ABC method, you rank tasks based on their importance and consequences. This way, you're not just reacting to what feels urgent but strategically handling what truly matters.

Let's blend these methods to supercharge your day. Start with items in the most urgent and important box of the Eisenhower Matrix—these are your A tasks. Work on those first. Once they're handled, move on to the Important but Not Urgent box—these become your B tasks. Finally, tackle the low-priority stuff from those other boxes, treating them as C tasks.

Think of it like managing a store. Urgent and Important tasks are like getting more supplies when you're running out. Important but

Not Urgent tasks are like planning a new product line—a bit more long-term but so essential. Urgent but Not Important tasks? That's like dealing with an upset customer about a small issue. Not a core function but needs handling. And that last group, the non-urgent and unimportant tasks—well, maybe those are just dusting the shelves again when there's no real need.

So, by recognizing what's really crucial and focusing your **energy** there, you make your **time** work for you instead of just filling it up with busy work. Simple? Sure. But really effective. Just imagine how you'll feel knocking out those A tasks and knowing you've done some serious work instead of just spinning your wheels. That's the **magic** of prioritization.

The Pomodoro Technique for Focused Work

Let's face it, **focusing** on tasks can be tough. So how do you keep that laser-like attention without wandering off? That's where setting **time limits** really helps.

Think of it this way: when you know you've only got a set amount of time to work, your brain kinda flips into high gear. It's like sprinting instead of jogging. It's easier to stay focused 'cause you know there's a break coming soon. It's like telling yourself, "You got this for just 25 minutes." That little **mind trick** works wonders.

So, how does the **Pomodoro Technique** fit into all this? It's pretty simple. You set a timer for 25 minutes to work on one task, and when the timer goes off, you take a 5-minute break. That's one Pomodoro. After four Pomodoros, you take a longer break, say 15-30 minutes. Easy, right?

This method helps in a couple of ways. First, it keeps you from burning out. Twenty-five minutes is long enough to make progress but short enough to not feel exhausting. Plus, those breaks in between keep your mind fresh. You're giving yourself little rewards after every sprint, which, in turn, keeps you **motivated** to start the next one.

Ever feel stuck before even starting a task? That's where the "5-minute rule" comes to the rescue. The idea here is that you commit to just 5 minutes of whatever you need to do. More often than not, you find it's easier to keep going than stopping. Sort of like getting into a pool; the hardest part is jumping in. But once you're in, swimming's not so bad.

I can't count how many times I've felt stuck but told myself, "Just five minutes." Almost every single time, I end up working far longer than that. It breaks that initial hesitation. So imagine combining this with the Pomodoro Technique. You're less likely to put things off 'cause, hey, what's 5 minutes? Just dive in and you might get into a good flow—thanks to that ticking clock. It's almost like your tiny **productivity** coach.

But wait, there's more. The whole structure of the Pomodoro Technique makes it easier to plan your day. Knowing you need a set number of Pomodoros for each task lets you break down bigger **projects** into bite-sized pieces. Conquering a mountain feels less scary when you're only worried about that first step or two.

Also, time limits prevent losing track of time, which helps you get more done without feeling frazzled. You end up with a solid block of focused work followed by a well-deserved short break. This manages fatigue and keeps the energy levels up across the day.

Multi-tasking often feels like making progress, but really, it just scatters your energy. Pomodoro pushes you to focus on one thing at a time. That single-minded attention boosts **quality**. Multi-tasking may ditch comfort zones, but it generally stirs up stress, aka evil productivity enemy.

So let's wrap it up. Setting time limits helps your brain stay in the zone, Pomodoro Technique organizes and energizes work sessions, and the 5-minute rule smashes the initial barriers. When you stitch all of it together, you'll find yourself getting more done and feeling less burned out.

Guess what? You're equipped with these simple skills for a more productive but not exhausting work strategy. Happy working!

Eliminating Time Wasters

Ever wonder where all your time goes? Sometimes it feels like the day slips through your fingers. That's where **time audits** come in. A time audit means tracking how you're spending every block of time throughout the day. Yeah, it sounds tedious, but it's super helpful. By doing a time audit, you can find out where you're **wasting** minutes or hours, through scrolling on social media or watching TV. This way, you know where the inefficiencies are hiding.

Think of it like this: Write down everything you do. Whether you're replying to emails, working on projects, or even making lunch, jot it all down. Most folks are shocked to see how much time is spent on things that aren't really important. Seeing it on paper makes it real. Trust me, it's like opening your eyes to a whole new way of understanding your day.

Now, once you know where your time's going, spotting and cutting down on wasteful activities becomes straightforward. For example, things like constantly checking your phone, endless email threads, or even overly long lunch breaks can sap your time. It's easy to think "Well, these are just little breaks." But added up, they become big chunks of wasted time.

To manage these **distractions**, put your phone on airplane mode during work hours. Another tip is clearing out unnecessary emails right when you get them, rather than letting them pile up. You'd be surprised how much more **efficient** you can be with a few simple changes like these.

Speaking of simple, let's introduce the "**two-minute rule**." This is a game-changer for handling tiny tasks. If a task takes less than two minutes, do it right away. It takes more energy to write a task down and schedule it in your planner than it does to just do it. Imagine this: a stack of papers on your desk, taking up mental space. Instead of planning a 'clean desk' hour later, you just spare those two minutes to clear them up. It frees your mind and reduces clutter.

Here's another relatable example: replying to emails. Say you get an email asking for a quick confirmation, and you end up putting it aside. Hours go by, and that email turns into a stressful open loop. Just taking seventy seconds to reply right away saves you the headache later.

Plus, implementing the two-minute rule serves as a **motivational** boost. You get quick wins, and it feels good to tick things off your list instantly. This encourages positive habits and really cements that sense of **discipline** we're aiming for.

Don't wait to adopt these habits. **Procrastination**—the arch-nemesis of self-discipline—feeds on delaying the inevitable. Spotting these bad habits and transforming them into productive ones can make a huge difference.

Got your notepad out yet? Note down where your time flies away, snip those wasteful activities, and tackle the small stuff right off the bat. Taking these simple steps helps in creating a day where every minute counts, contributing toward achieving your bigger goals without detracting from your brainpower.

You've got plenty of tools now—time audits, spotting time-wasters, and the two-minute rule. Your day just got a whole lot more productive and disciplined. Ready to kick those time wasters out the door?

Creating Effective Daily Routines

Getting your **mornings** and **evenings** right can set the tone for your entire day. Think about it: Mornings are your launchpad. If they're chaotic and rushed, the rest of your day can feel off. So, setting a solid morning routine is like putting the right fuel in your tank. On the other hand, evening routines help you wind down. It's your chance to reflect, relax, and get ready for the next day. Together, they act like bookends, stabilizing your whole day.

Now, everyone's different. Your best friend might be a morning person, ready to sprint at the crack of dawn. But maybe you're more of a night owl. And that's okay! The key is to tailor your **routines** to fit your own energy levels and productivity patterns.

To start, figure out when you're most alert and when you're sluggish. If you're not sure, keep a journal for a week. Jot down when you feel most productive and when you feel like you're dragging. This can give you some pretty clear clues.

Let's say you've figured out that you're sharpest in the evening. Maybe your most challenging tasks should go there. Use mornings for activities that don't require as much brainpower, like planning your day or answering emails. Aligning your tasks with your energy levels makes things feel way easier.

Once you have your basic outline, start thinking about what repetitive tasks you could turn into **habits**. Enter "habit stacking."

Habit stacking is like adding new habits on top of existing ones. Imagine you already brush your teeth every morning (I hope you do!). While brushing, why not think about three things you're grateful for? You've just stacked 'reflecting on gratitude' on top of 'brushing teeth.' It becomes natural over time.

Here's how you can stack habits:

• **Identify Anchor Habits** - These are things you already do without thinking, like making coffee or getting dressed.

• **Attach New Habits to These Anchors** - Use the momentum of your anchor habits to support new ones. For example, do five push-ups while your coffee brews.

• **Repeat Daily** - Consistency is key. The more often you do it, the more automatic it becomes.

Try to keep it simple at first. Complicating your routine can make it harder to stick to, and you don't want to set yourself up for failure.

Let's bring it all together. If mornings are your high-energy times, your routine could include a **workout**, a productive planning session, and a balanced breakfast. In the evenings, when you're settling down, you might journal, read a book, and prep for the next day.

Consistency will eventually smooth out the rough edges. You'll start feeling more control over your day just by mastering these bookends. This isn't some "one-size-fits-all" fix, but more of a custom-made solution for your life.

Give it a shot. Tailor your routines to your energy levels, and use habit stacking to make the process easier. Your days will start to look different—more structured, less chaotic. And you might surprise yourself with how much more you get done.

Practical Exercise: Time Audit and Optimization

Ready to get real about how you spend your time? Here's a challenge for you: **track** everything you do for a whole week. Yep, everything.

From the moment you **wake** up till you hit the hay, jot down when you start and stop each activity. Glance at your watch or phone and note those minutes. Sounds like a pain? Well, it kinda is, but trust me, it's worth it. Think of yourself as a detective in your own life. What are you really up to all day? Where's all that time **slipping** away?

Once you've got a week's worth of data, it's time to **sort** everything into three buckets—essential, productive, and non-productive. Let me break it down for you:

• Essential activities: These are the must-dos like eating, sleeping, working (if you've got a job), or studying (if you're hitting the books). The stuff you gotta do to keep on keepin' on.

• Productive activities: These are the tasks that **push** you closer to your goals. Think working out, reading something that makes you smarter, or those moments when you're totally in the zone getting stuff done.

• Non-productive activities: Pretty much everything else. Mindlessly scrolling through social media, binge-watching TV shows, or just lounging around doing nothing special.

Now, grab a calculator and **crunch** those numbers. Add up the time you spent in each category over the week. You can probably see where this is headed, right? How big is that non-productive slice of the pie? Be real with yourself.

Notice any patterns? Maybe you're spending way too much time on Instagram. Or huddled up for hours watching Netflix. No need to beat yourself up—we all do it. It's just time to spot those sneaky time **drains**.

So, what's next? Set some personal goals to trim down that wasted time. Maybe decide to cap social media at an hour a day, or watch just two episodes of a show instead of powering through a whole season.

Now, **remap** your schedule, making sure there's more space for the essential and productive stuff. It doesn't have to be perfect. Aim for a balance that leaves room for both the things that spark joy and boost productivity.

Give this new schedule a whirl for a week—just as an experiment. Keep tabs on your thoughts and feelings about it. Does it feel rushed or stressful? Or maybe the opposite, giving you more breathing room?

After the week's up, fine-tune that schedule based on what you discovered. If you felt too pressed for time, maybe you need some wiggle room here and there. Or, if you found an extra pocket of time where none existed before, hey, that's a win!

A time audit won't solve all of life's mysteries, but it helps you see where your hours and minutes are really going. Think of it as refocusing the lens you view your days through. And trust me, if you stick with it, you'll find yourself wondering why you never did this earlier.

In Conclusion

This chapter has armed you with the **essential** skills and techniques needed to effectively **manage** your time and boost your self-discipline. By breaking down complex concepts into manageable tips, it aims to make you more **productive** and organized in both your personal and professional life.

In this chapter, you've picked up some valuable insights. You've learned the importance of distinguishing between urgent and important tasks. The **Eisenhower Matrix** has been introduced as a nifty tool to help you **prioritize** tasks effectively. You've also discovered how the **Pomodoro Technique** can send your focus and productivity through the roof.

Time audits have been highlighted as key in sniffing out and cutting down on inefficiencies in your daily routines. You've also explored how designing effective daily **routines** can set a positive tone for your day from sunrise to bedtime.

By putting these strategies into practice, you can expect to see some serious improvements in how you **manage** your time. Remember, the secret sauce to success is in consistently applying these techniques. Keep tweaking your approach, and you'll surely smash your **goals** with a disciplined mindset.

I'm confident that if you stick with these methods, you'll see a real difference in how you tackle your day-to-day life. So go ahead, give it a shot, and watch your productivity soar!

Chapter 7: Developing a Disciplined Mindset

Ever wonder what sets the doers apart from the dreamers? Is it some secret **success** formula that only a few know? I've thought a lot about these questions. And honestly, it all boils down to one thing—a **disciplined** mindset. But don't go thinking it's some unattainable ideal. You, yes you, can change how you think and make real changes.

It's like you're about to embark on a journey to tweak your thinking habits. You'll discover techniques that'll help you become more disciplined. Curious? You'll soon realize that what you might see as limitations are just misconceptions. Want to know what's stopping you from pushing past those **comfort** zones? It's not what you think, trust me.

You'll play around with things like positive self-talk and using **affirmations** that aren't cheesy, I promise. Ever heard of the 40% rule? It's a game-changer for sure—let's just say you'll amaze yourself with what you're capable of. And you'll wrap it all up with a mindset shift **journaling** exercise that isn't just fluff; it's practical stuff that works.

Brace yourself—you're gonna want to dig into the whole chapter once you catch a glimpse of what's possible. You'll explore ways to **overcome** obstacles, push your limits, and tap into your hidden potential. This isn't about becoming someone else; it's about becoming the best version of yourself.

Remember, developing a disciplined mindset isn't about perfection. It's about progress. You'll learn to embrace challenges as opportunities for **growth** and see setbacks as stepping stones. With each page, you'll uncover new strategies to **strengthen** your mental resilience and sharpen your focus.

So, are you ready to unlock your full potential? Dive in, and let's transform your mindset together. The journey to a more disciplined you starts now.

Cognitive Restructuring for Self-Discipline

Let's talk about what messes with your self-discipline: cognitive distortions. These distortions are just silly ways your **brain** tricks you into thinking bad stuff that's not even true. It's like your mind is playing pranks on you. You've got to figure out what these tricks are so you can stop getting played.

Ever notice how sometimes you think stuff like, "I'll never get this done," or "I always mess up?" Those are classic cognitive distortions. They mess with your head and tell you all these negative things, making **discipline** nearly impossible. You're more likely to quit if you think you always fail, right? So it's super important to shut down these distortions before they get in your way.

How do you spot them? Well, next time you're frustrated or thinking you can't do something, pay attention. What exactly are you telling yourself? Stuff like "This always happens to me" or "I'm so stupid" are major red flags. Your brain exaggerates. It takes one bad moment and blows it up, making it feel like it's been this way forever.

Once you've spotted these bad **thoughts**, you've got to challenge them. Ask yourself, is this really true? Like, really true? Often, it's not. You're probably thinking these exaggerated thoughts because your **emotions** are running high. Separate feelings from facts. Feeling bummed out doesn't mean you're a failure.

Let's get a bit hands-on. If your brain's going, "I'm such a loser," question it. Why would you be? Did one mistake suddenly erase all your past accomplishments? Probably not. Flip that thought and remind yourself of times you succeeded. Balance the scales.

Now, for the "thought stopping" trick. Think of it like hitting a big pause button on a bad TV show. As soon as a bad thought pops up— "Ugh, I'm never good enough!"—mentally yell, "Stop!" Visualize a stop sign if you need to. Immediately shift your **focus** to something positive or neutral. The more you practice this, the better you'll get at it.

Some people find it really useful to actually say "Stop!" out loud. If you're in a place where that's not too weird, give it a try. Interrupt the flow of negative thoughts. Replace them with something good.

Once you've stopped a bad thought, cross-examine it. Was it even worth thinking about? Often, it's something you can let go of. Fill your mind with thoughts that uplift you. Instead of letting your brain run wild with bad stories, feed it good ones. You control the **narrative**.

In summary, cognitive distortions screw up your self-discipline. Recognizing these bad thoughts for what they are is step one. Calling them out by challenging their truth is step two. And finally, shutting those thoughts down with the "thought stopping" trick can keep you on track. So, check your thoughts, question them, and then stop 'em dead in their tracks. You've got the **power** to discipline your mind and, in turn, your **life**.

Positive Self-Talk and Affirmations

Have you ever noticed how the way you **talk** to yourself can change how you **feel** and what you do? When you mess up something simple, and suddenly you're saying stuff like, "I'm so useless" or "I'll never get this right," that kind of negative self-talk can drag you down. It crushes **motivation** and makes it way harder to stick to your goals. But here's the thing: if you flip that script, it can totally change the game. Imagine telling yourself, "I can handle this," or, "Every mistake is just another step toward getting better." Feels nice, right?

Positive self-talk isn't just about being all sunshine and rainbows. It's about being kind and supportive to yourself, even when you don't necessarily feel like it. Say you're trying to break a bad **habit** like procrastinating. Instead of beating yourself up for not getting things done, you say, "Alright, let's take it one step at a time. I've got what it takes to finish this." That change in mindset can be the push you need to keep going.

Now, on to **affirmations**. These are like little pep talks you give yourself. The cool thing about affirmations is that they work best when they're personal. So, you want to craft ones that speak to your particular situation. Start with something that's true or that you want to be true. If you're shooting to be more organized, say, "I am a person who gets things done." Or, maybe you want to be more confident: "I have the skills and talents to achieve my goals." When you say these affirmations regularly, you're reprogramming your brain to believe them. And, over time, you start acting like that person.

There's a simple way to practice positive self-talk that's super effective—the mirror **technique**. Here's how it works:

- Stand in front of a mirror where you can see yourself.

- Look yourself in the eye. This part's important.

- Talk to yourself with affirmations. Out loud. It might feel weird at first—like really weird. But trust me, it's worth it.

- Say your affirmations with belief. Even if you don't fully believe them yet, pretend like you do.

It's like giving your brain a heads-up that this is who you are or who you're becoming. Over time, your mind catches up with your words. The mirror technique also helps build self-**confidence**. Seeing yourself declare your strengths and positive attributes makes you start viewing yourself in that light.

Also, regular **practice** is what amplifies the effect. Put it in your daily routine. Brushing your teeth? Do a quick session. About to head out for the day? Another quick session. Soon, standing in front of a mirror telling yourself how awesome you are will be as routine as having your morning coffee (or tea, if that's your thing).

To wrap it up—self-talk, positive affirmations, mirror technique—they're simple but powerful tools. They help pave the way for boosting your self-discipline. Start with kind words to yourself, create your own personalized affirmations, and don't shy away from talking to your reflection. Give it a shot. You might just find that you're way stronger and more **resilient** than you thought.

The 40% Rule: Pushing Beyond Perceived Limits

Ever feel like you've hit a wall and couldn't keep going? Well, what if I told you that you've probably got loads more left in the tank? There's this idea called the 40% Rule. Basically, it means that when you think you're done, like you can't go any further, you're really only at 40% of what's actually **possible** for you. Crazy, right?

Think of your brain as having this safety switch. It kicks in when things get tough, convincing you to stop to avoid pain or discomfort. This is where mental backups come into play. They're like your brain's way of saying, "Whoa, that's enough for today!" These mental backups connect to both your perceived physical and mental **limits**, making you believe you've reached your cap when in reality, you've still got a long way to go.

So how can you spot signs you're about to give up too soon? Well, you might start feeling overwhelmingly tired even if you haven't been at it long. Self-doubt might creep in, saying stuff like, "I can't do this." You might even start to rationalize why quitting is okay.

When these pop up, it's time to **push** through. One trick is the "micro-goal setting" technique. It sounds super simple because, well... it is.

When I say micro-goal, I mean really tiny steps. Doing fifty pushups might seem impossible right now, but ten? Not too bad. So instead of focusing on the end result, break it up. Aim to hit another micro-goal first, then another, and another.

It's a bit like tricking your brain. By focusing on smaller tasks, you're not as overwhelmed. You know, something like saying to yourself, "I'll just read one more page" instead of "I have to read this whole big book." Baby goals not only make anything more manageable but also give you that sweet sense of **accomplishment** time and time again.

Sometimes, it helps to kind of visualize it too—you know, just one more driveway's length if you're running, one more dish if you're cleaning. Small wins keep you moving forward, and before you know it, you're way past the limit you thought you had.

Remember that moment when self-doubt whispers you can't go any further? That's your cue to push just a tad more. This sin of "giving up too soon" hides in all sorts of small decisions every day. Done cooking after chopping veg. Cleaning but leaving mail scattered. Half-finished plans.

Sweat the small stuff. Push just one more step each time you hit a micro-goal, especially when the **force** to quit feels the strongest. Whether it's an essay, a chore schedule, or marathon training, those small extra ticks around set limits make mountains eventually.

Now, think about the last project where you stopped early. You likely defaulted to planned mental stops. Fight those 'finished' triggers by carving extra time for mundane tasks into achievements. Bust barriers with minutes bolstered by slight consecutive pushes. Winning becomes a straightforward cumulative of habit, a little longer tension, a small add within doable range translating relentless expansion through practical routine scripts conditioned over comfort cushioning signatures backing ease.

Apply the consistent micro-step overcoming lens, and dedicated gaps appear to shrink into incremental fields. Next time rough patches plot to halt your **advancement**, chip away at those chokeholds against mental block signifiers. Thread omnidirectional multiform standards into noteworthy moment-accomplishing extension. Reframe setbacks needing micro-bar operational ladder surges into soft stacking determined evaluative firm flourished endeavors.

Those retreat urges signify disciplined, bridging away perceived constraints mentally handed physiology bug fixation traps willing residential accounted resilient grasps sustainable reassurance rosters guide broader buffering continual declared standard-fitting prowess behavioral compounds.

Reckon mental backups execute thwart, altogether summoning stacked reinclined perpetual pathways reinforcing reclaimed inclusions opstap adapting reach spanning intra-crux responsive redesigns scrutinized turned flail mechanisms conditioning refinished perceived resume inquiries interpreting causal residual passing optimized strain gathered redesigned intersect pathways bridging surged retaining inclusive overcoming largescale back satisfaction interminably accompanying flair transitioning modicum movecharacter spearheads concludes semantic cool redivinity reaffirm spurred soft dynamics nodded seeking outlaw directed structurally pooling life's productive beyond defined ready **horizons**.

Keep pressing... You've always got this!

Overcoming Self-Limiting Beliefs

Let's dive into these pesky self-limiting beliefs and how they mess with your head. Ever wonder why you sometimes just can't stick to your **goals**? Maybe you were all pumped about hitting the gym every day but somehow ended up binge-watching a whole series instead. Self-limiting beliefs sneak in when you're about to make changes. They form based on past experiences, failures, and what other people have told you over the years. These beliefs get anchored in your mind, and you start to believe them like they're set in stone. They tell you things like, "I'm not smart enough," or "I can't do this." And boy, do they screw up your self-discipline.

When you buy into these beliefs, you're **sabotaging** yourself. For example, believing you're terrible at public speaking can make your palms sweat and your voice shake, making it even harder to speak up. Or think about that belief you've got – that you're just not cut out for leadership roles. Instead of trying and maybe failing, you just sit back and let other people take the lead.

But here's the deal – you can spot these beliefs. Yeah, really. You just need to tune into your inner **dialogue**. Catch yourself whenever you say "I can't" or "I'm not." Ask yourself why you think that. Did something happen in the past? Did someone tell you you weren't good enough? Challenge those thoughts. Like, really question them.

A cool trick I like to use is collecting **evidence**. Picture yourself as a detective collecting clues about why this belief isn't true. Start jotting down things you've done well – moments you've succeeded when you didn't think you would. Maybe it's that time you aced a presentation at work, even though you were shaking in your shoes. Or you managed to stick to a diet plan when all the odds were against you. Find every piece of proof that discredits your "I can't" belief.

Next, write those down and keep that list somewhere you can peek at often. Build on it, too. Got a new win? Add it to your collection of evidence.

Usually, you don't even question these limiting beliefs. They just sit there in the background, making you think you're not capable. Looking for solid evidence—and I mean solid evidence—can shift your **perspective**. Feel that "I can't manage my time" belief staring you down? Look for moments when you actually did manage it well. Stories you've heard might fuel these limiting thoughts too. "You'll never succeed in this industry, it's brutal." Guess what? Dive into examples where you or others proved that wrong.

In your day-to-day life, these beliefs also affect how **disciplined** you are. Say you believe you're inherently disorganized. That belief could become a crutch. Simple things like setting goals or planning out your day get harder. Discarding those self-limiting beliefs frees you from those mental cages. It's bizarre – you start spotting opportunities where you thought there were none.

Wrapping your head around this means embracing the idea that beliefs are often just old stories, nagging at you without real proof. Once you pick away at these mental **barriers**, anything's possible. It's a tough task – nobody's saying it's quick. But wouldn't you want to step out of that mental quicksand?

So next time you catch yourself in one of these thinking traps, play detective. Gather that evidence. Make a list, highlight it in neon if you have to, and knock those beliefs down. Because you're **capable** – no second thoughts about it!

Practical Exercise: Mindset Shift Journaling

Ready to shake things up with some mindset shift journaling? This exercise might just become your new **best friend** on the path to better self-discipline. Let's dive in!

First, think about a **belief** that's holding you back from practicing self-discipline. This kind of sticky thought often sneaks in when you doubt yourself or lack confidence. It could be something like, "I'm just not a disciplined person," or, "I always procrastinate." Got it? Great, let's keep going.

Now, jot down any **proof** you can think of that totally contradicts this limiting belief. Maybe there was a time when you nailed a tough task. Or perhaps you managed to stick to a small routine, even if it was just brushing your teeth every morning. Look for evidence that shows you can actually be disciplined when you set your mind to it.

Next, come up with a new **belief statement** that's positive and empowering. Something you want to believe about yourself. Make it strong but feel true to you. It could be, "I can develop self-discipline," or, "I'm capable of building good habits."

List specific **actions** you can take that align with this new belief. Think day-to-day things you can actually do. It might be setting a goal to wake up early every day, creating a daily to-do list, or dedicating 15 minutes each day to a habit you want to form. Keep it practical.

Every day, take a moment to journal about things that support your new positive belief. It could be noting when you followed through on your plans for the day or any little wins that show you're on the right track. See those small victories? Write 'em down.

Keep tabs on the times you acted on your new belief. Make a note or use a simple checkmark system in your journal. Did you stick to your new bedtime? Did you complete your morning routine? Record it.

Each week, reflect on how your thoughts and **actions** have changed. Have you been sticking to your new habits? How do you feel about your new belief? Write down your thoughts and notice any changes in how you approach self-discipline now.

A month later, think about how things are going. Make any adjustments based on your reflections. Maybe certain actions worked well while others didn't. It's all a learning process, so tweak and continue doing what works best for you.

Through all of this, keep it simple and **consistent**. And really give it your honest try for a month. Journaling can do wonders—it's like having your own personal coach.

So, let's harness the power of your mind, put it on paper, and see where it leads. Start right now... Seriously, grab that pen!

In Conclusion

You've now got some **powerful** tools for developing a disciplined mindset. By putting what you've learned into action, you can better **manage** your thoughts, foster positive self-talk, push beyond your limits, overcome self-limiting beliefs, and practice effective exercises. These strategies can **guide** you toward your goals and better self-discipline habits. Here are the key points to remember:

You've learned about cognitive distortions and how they can negatively **impact** your self-discipline. It's crucial to identify and challenge negative thought patterns that hold you back. Positive self-talk and creating personalized affirmations can give your **motivation** a boost. The "40% Rule" shows you that you've got more in you than you think, helping you push past perceived limits. Recognizing and challenging self-limiting beliefs is vital for personal **growth** and better discipline.

By putting these techniques to work, you can cultivate a stronger, more disciplined mindset. Use them to overcome challenges, break away from negativity, and achieve your goals. Every step you take toward better discipline makes you stronger and more resilient, **empowering** you to realize your true potential. The journey to self-discipline starts now. Stay dedicated and keep believing in the process—you're capable of **greatness**!

Chapter 8: Building Resilience and Grit

Ever wondered why some folks seem to **bounce** back no matter what? I ask myself that all the time. You might think it's just luck, but it's really not. It's **grit**. It's mental **toughness**. It's the stuff that you can learn and develop. In this chapter, we're going to explore how you can turn your setbacks into **comebacks** and manage stress like a pro.

I've faced more than a few rough patches in life—moments when giving up felt like the easiest route. But guess what? Those **struggles** become the stepping stones for growth. I'm here to share some of the lessons I've gathered along the way in a way that's relatable and actionable for you. You're not alone.

Imagine reaching a point where no challenge feels too big. Where you don't crumble under **pressure** but stand tall, knowing you've got the tools to get through it. That's what mental toughness does. It allows you to **persevere** even when things get tough. In this chapter, you'll uncover stress management tricks and find practical exercises designed to build your **resilience**.

It's time to become the unstoppable force you've always wanted to be. Ready? Let's dive in!

Developing Mental Toughness Through Challenges

Let's talk about stress inoculation. It might sound **complicated**, but it's not so bad. Think of it like a mental vaccine. Just as a tiny bit of a virus in a vaccine makes your body stronger against the real thing, a bit of stress toughens your mind. By putting yourself in slightly stressful situations, you teach your brain to handle bigger stressors.

So, what's this stress inoculation really about? You start small. Begin with a manageable task that **stresses** you just a little. Maybe it's speaking up in a meeting when you'd rather stay quiet. Over time, your brain gets used to these small challenges—and the bigger ones don't seem so scary anymore. Plus, each success builds **confidence**. You start thinking, "Hey, I handled that. I can handle this too."

Getting used to tough situations slowly is key. Imagine you're at the gym. You wouldn't start with heavyweights on day one. You'd begin with the light ones—working up as you get stronger. It's the same with mental **resilience**.

Start with small challenges that push you out of your comfort zone. For example, stay calm when you miss public transport instead of getting upset. Over time, handle things that take just a bit more mental muscle—like having a hard conversation with a friend. With each step, you're teaching your brain that you can manage more than you thought.

Now, let's chat about something cool called 'comfort zone expansion.' It's like one of those stretching exercises but for your mind. First, figure out what scares or worries you—a **presentation**, talking to strangers, or maybe traveling alone. Start by doing something less scary but related to it. If the thought of speaking in front of a crowd terrifies you, start by talking in small groups. Or, just practice speaking up more in regular one-on-one conversations. The idea is to challenge yourself just a little beyond what feels safe. Slowly, that comfort zone gets bigger, and what scared you before doesn't seem so terrifying.

Here's a little trick I like. Face small fears in your daily life. Afraid of being alone? Spend an afternoon by yourself doing something you enjoy. Nervous about meeting new people? Say hello to someone new in your neighborhood or at work. This isn't about jumping into the fire; it's about getting close enough to feel some heat without getting burned. The **reward** here? You end each week a bit braver than before.

In my opinion, once you've got the hang of embracing little challenges, life gets a bit more interesting. You look at tough situations not as things to avoid but as ways to prove to yourself how **tough** you really are. And before you know it, things that once seemed impossible start feeling, well, possible.

That's it in a nutshell. Handle stress a little at a time, push your limits gradually, and soon, your 'can'ts' will begin to turn into 'cans.' It's all about building that mental **toughness** one challenge at a time.

Bouncing Back from Setbacks

Ever felt like the universe had it out for you when things don't go your way? It's tempting to just throw your hands up and say, "Why bother?" But hang on a second. **Failures** aren't the end of the road; they're just a detour. In fact, it's crucial to see these hiccups as golden chances to soak up some wisdom.

It's all about **mindset**. When something doesn't work out, don't beat yourself up. See it as a learning opportunity. Every setback has lessons hidden in there, just waiting to be discovered. Why, you ask? Because every failure teaches you what not to do next time. Think of it like discovering which light switches don't turn on the light. Eventually, you'll find the right one. Each attempt you make, you're gathering info about what works and what doesn't.

But how do you pull useful lessons from your failures? Simple. Look back at what went wrong. Not in a self-pitying kind of way, but with a curious mind. Ask yourself, "What could I have done differently?" or "What did I miss?" This **reflection** isn't about finding where you failed, but how you can do better next time. It's like doing a post-match analysis after a game: why didn't that play work out? What was the other team doing that ensured their win? Learn, adjust, and keep going.

One trick to keep a positive vibe during tough times is the "three good things" exercise. When you're feeling low, just grab a pen and paper (or your phone) and jot down three things that went well today. Doesn't have to be anything earth-shattering—maybe your morning coffee was on point, or you caught up with an old friend. The idea is to focus on the good stuff, no matter how small. This helps you notice little wins even during rough patches, kinda like finding small gems in the dirt.

Keeping a positive **attitude** doesn't make the stumbling blocks disappear. It just shrinks their impact on your mental outlook. When you're naturally leaning towards finding the good, setbacks don't seem as gigantic.

I remember a time when I bombed a big presentation. I was crushed. But instead of letting that struck-through moment break me, I looked back. I saw that I wasn't well-prepared and got caught off-guard by some questions. So, next time, I planned better and tried to think, 'What might they ask me?' This not only made me better at presenting but also built my **resilience**.

It's normal to sulk a bit post-failure. But it's what you do after the sulking that matters. Dive back into the scene with sharper eyes and a stronger mind. Keep your chin up, use every setback as a training ground for your success, and soon, bouncing back will be second nature. Got it?

Let's wrap this up with a little emphasis on **grit**. It's like building muscle. A withdrawal here, some pain there, but you get stronger every rep you make. So go ahead, wear your past failures with pride. They're simply proof that you're daring enough to try. And that, my friend, is the mark of true **resilience**.

The Power of Perseverance

Alright, let's chat about **grit**. It's that special blend of passion and persistence you need to achieve those long-term goals. Why grit? Because life isn't a sprint—it's a marathon full of hurdles and detours. You need grit to keep running when you're exhausted, to keep pushing when times get tough. Grit isn't just about working hard; it's about hanging in there through thick and thin.

So, how does it help you stick with things? Think about this: having **passion** for what you do and staying motivated over long stretches. Got a goal to get fit? Great! Enthusiastic at first? Definitely. But then the initial excitement fades. Here's where grit kicks in. It's the steady effort you put in every day, those morning jogs, and skipping that extra slice of pizza, that leads you to your goal. No shortcuts. Just consistent, often unglamorous, hard work.

Picture a mountain. Grit helps you climb it, step by step—even when it feels like you're not going anywhere. Each step, each stumble makes you stronger. And gradually, you find yourself closer to the summit.

Next up, let's build a **growth mindset**. Simple idea—believing you can improve. If you think your abilities are set in stone, you'll give up easily. "I can't do it" becomes your mantra. But with a growth mindset, every obstacle is a chance to learn and grow. Think of each failure as a stepping stone. Flunked a test? Study harder. Didn't get the job? Tweak your resume and try again.

How to keep pushing through? Start by changing how you talk to yourself. When you're faced with a setback, ask, "What can I learn from this?" Not, "Why me?" Small shift, big difference. Surround yourself with people who challenge and support you. Cheer for their successes, and let them cheer for you. A hunger for improvement pushes you further.

Okay, onto staying **motivated**. Big dreams don't come overnight, and that's why small wins matter. They're like those little signposts along a never-ending road trip. They tell you you're on the right track. Want to run a marathon? Start by running a mile. Celebrate that mile. You doubled your savings? Pat yourself on the back.

Set mini-goals. Say you want to write a book. Goal? Write a chapter a week. Not so daunting that way, right? Every mini-goal you achieve fuels your fire, keeps you going. And don't forget the joy they bring. Small victories make the grind bearable.

How do you tap into this power of small wins? Break your tasks into smaller, manageable chunks. Get into the habit of ticking things off your to-do list. It feels good, doesn't it? Tackle each small task with the same gusto as a big project. Each step forward, no matter how tiny, is **progress**.

To connect the dots, grit keeps you moving, growth mindset fine-tunes your approach, and small wins keep your spirit up. Together, they help you power through. You build a cycle of effort, learning, and rewards that sustain you through thick and thin.

So there you have it, **grit**, **growth mindset**, and **small wins** are your allies. Hold onto them as you chase those dreams.

Stress Management Techniques

Stress **messes** with your self-control big time. When you're always stressed out, you just can't think straight. Your mind gets foggy, and making good decisions feels like a Herculean task. It's why you might binge-eat junk food when you're swamped at work or blow off exercising when you're too worried about other stuff. Long-term stress basically kicks your self-discipline to the curb.

So how do you find out what **stresses** you out? Watch yourself. Think about the last time you felt completely overwhelmed. What started it? Was it too many deadlines at work? Family drama? Knowing your stress triggers means you can plan for them beforehand. Thinking ahead can save your sanity. Stressed about a big presentation next week? It might be a good idea to practice your speech a little bit every day instead of cramming the night before. These small steps help de-stress.

And man, let's not forget about dealing with stress in the moment. Sometimes you need something that works fast. Ever heard of box **breathing**? It's pretty neat and super simple. You're gonna love it because it's great at calming you down on the spot. Here's what you do: Breathe in deeply for a count of four, hold your breath for four counts, exhale for another four counts, and then hold it again for four counts. Repeat this a few times, and it's like a fast pick-me-up for your brain. Next time traffic's driving you nuts or your to-do list looks like a bad joke, try box breathing. You'll feel a lot better, promise.

Spending time figuring out what sets you off stress-wise and how you can prep ahead of time makes stress less scary. It's like preparing for a test. The more you know what's coming, the less **intimidating** it gets. Keep an eye on your typical "freak out" situations and think up some go-to solutions. You'll get better at it with time.

And if you feel swamped, tackle one thing at a time. You'll feel less like tearing your hair out if you focus on small wins. Whether it's finishing a couple of tasks out of ten or just getting through a particularly rough hour, baby steps count.

Last but not least, give box breathing a real shot. You won't believe how something so simple can turn your day around. Next time you're **freaking** out, breathe in that box pattern. It's a go-to hack for cutting stress down to size. Keep practicing and it becomes second nature.

Self-control is like a **muscle**. The more you train it, the stronger it gets. Handle that stress better and everything else will start to feel way easier. And hey, practice makes perfect, right? So your homework is just that: Spot what stresses you out, come up with a plan, and use box breathing to chill out when you need it most.

Practical Exercise: Resilience-Building Activities

Let's dive right into **building** that grit. The aim here is to stretch your comfort zone and boost **resilience** step by step. Where better to start than by picking a challenging **goal**? Choose something that'll push you, but not so hard that you burn out. Maybe it's running a certain distance, finishing a book, or even learning a new skill. This goal should make you a tad uncomfortable but still seem doable with some effort.

Now, take that goal and break it into bite-sized chunks. These smaller steps are your daily **tasks**. If your goal is running 5 kilometers and you're a couch potato, don't sweat it. Start by aiming to run just 1 kilometer or even just walk for a bit. The idea is to get moving, not to be perfect right away.

Promise yourself you'll take one small step every day for a week. Just one. It can be tiny. Say your goal is learning a new language. Spend ten minutes each day practicing vocabulary or listening to a native speaker. Not too bad, right?

Day by day, jot down what happens. Write about how you felt during the **activity**, what was tough, what wasn't, and any insights you had. Feel free to rant a little. This not only helps you make sense of your progress but also gives you a record of your journey to look back on. It's like keeping your own diary of growth.

After a week, take a glance over your notes. How'd it go? Any surprising hiccups or easy victories? Use this feedback to tweak your approach. If five minutes of practice was too easy, bump it up to ten. If it was tough, maybe stick to five but make sure you're laser-focused. It's totally fine to adjust based on what you've learned.

Once things start feeling a bit easier, gradually make your daily challenges tougher. If you've been walking, maybe start jogging. If you've been spending ten minutes on a new language, increase it to fifteen. It's all about pushing the boundaries a little more day by day.

And hey, don't forget to celebrate your **wins**. Did you complete all seven days of tiny steps? That's awesome! Give yourself a pat on the back. But also take a look at any setbacks. Hit a snag mid-week? Great, that's a learning opportunity. Dig into why it happened and how you can avoid it later on. Growth comes as much from facing mistakes as from celebrating successes.

Keep this process going for a month. Each week, reflect, tweak things, push a bit harder. By the end of the month, you'll have stretched your resilience and expanded your comfort zone. You'll probably surprise yourself with how much **progress** you've made. And the experiences and lessons from this will act like stepping stones for your next goal. It's all about building resilience, bit by bit.

So go ahead. Pick that challenge, break it into tiny steps, and show off a bit of grit. This isn't just about smashing a goal. It's about building that internal strength and stamina that will serve you across all areas of life. Ready? Let's do it.

In Conclusion

This chapter has provided valuable **insights** about building resilience and grit. You've explored how to develop mental **toughness** through challenges, bounce back from setbacks, understand the power of **perseverance**, manage stress, and practice resilience-building exercises. Here's a quick refresher to inspire you to apply these lessons in your own life.

You've seen how facing stress can build mental toughness through stress inoculation. You've learned to use the comfort zone expansion technique for growing **confidence**. The chapter highlighted the importance of viewing failures as opportunities to learn. You've discovered that **grit** is key to long-term success and how a growth mindset can boost perseverance. You've also picked up effective stress management techniques, like identifying **triggers** and using box breathing.

Now it's time to put these strategies and techniques into practice in your daily life to strengthen your **resilience** and grit. You're capable of achieving remarkable things when you take small, consistent steps forward. Keep challenging yourself, learn from your experiences, and celebrate your progress to build a robust and resilient mindset. You've got what it takes to **succeed**, one step at a time!

Chapter 9: The Role of Physical Health in Self-Discipline

Ever wondered why some days you feel like you can **conquer** the world, while others you can't seem to peel yourself off the couch? It's not just you. There's a fascinating **connection** between your physical health and your ability to stick to your goals. This chapter's journey is all about unraveling this link and showing you how to **harness** it for self-discipline.

There's something magical about understanding your **body**. By tuning into your **nutrition**, finding the right exercise routine, and optimizing your sleep, you can create an inner powerhouse. I'm not just talking theories here. You'll find a practical exercise that helps you put this all together into a holistic health plan. I've realized that small changes in how you care for your body can have big payoffs in self-discipline.

You're gonna be amazed, seriously. Trust the process, and reap the **benefits**. Ever felt that surge of willpower after a good workout? Or the laser focus that comes with a rested mind? Yeah, it's all connected. So are you ready to see a new level of self-control? Dive in. You might just find the key to becoming the best **version** of yourself.

Remember, it's not about perfection, but progress. By making small, consistent **improvements** in your physical health, you're setting yourself up for success in all areas of life. So, let's get started on this journey to a healthier, more disciplined you!

Nutrition and Its Impact on Willpower

Ever felt like you've hit a **brain fog** mid-afternoon? Well, it's no fluke. It's all about blood sugar levels and how they impact your mind. When you eat something sweet, your blood sugar spikes. This boost can make you feel alert and full of energy. But it's a short-lived buzz. Soon enough, your blood sugar will drop like a rock. And with it, your focus and **willpower** go downhill fast. Keeping your blood sugar stable means your brain works better—think of it like giving your car the right fuel so it runs smoothly.

So, how do you keep that blood sugar stable? Keep it simple. A **balanced diet** is key. Try to spread your meals and snacks evenly throughout the day. You want a good mix of carbs, proteins, and fats. Carb-loaded foods like white bread or pasta can lead to those big spikes and crashes. Instead, go for whole grains, veggies, and fruits. These release energy slowly. Protein, like chicken or beans, helps keep you full and balances your blood sugar. Healthy fats from avocados or nuts add a steady stream of fuel for your brain. It's like building a house; you need sturdy, reliable materials to keep it standing strong.

Want an easy way to plan your meals? Let's chat about the "**plate method**." Imagine your plate is a pie chart. Half of it should be filled with veggies—think of greens, peppers, and carrots. A quarter goes to your protein—like chicken, tofu, or fish. The last quarter can be for carbs—whole grains like quinoa or brown rice. If you need a little more help, add a side of fruit and a dairy or dairy alternative. This simple way of dividing up your meal helps keep everything balanced. Your meals will be more nutritious, and you'll find it easier to keep your focus and resist cravings.

You've probably heard the saying, "You are what you eat." It's pretty spot-on here. Eating **junk food**, loaded with sugars and unhealthy fats, messes with your mental gears. You become more prone to emotional swings, and your self-control takes a nosedive. Slow and steady wins the race. Opt for meals that will keep you on an even keel throughout the day, and your willpower will thank you. Instead of snacking on chips, reach for some almonds. Swap out that soda for water or herbal tea. It's about small changes that lead to big shifts in your mental game.

In summary, what you eat directly impacts how well your **brain** works and how much **self-discipline** you can muster. By choosing a balanced diet, spreading your meals out, and using handy tools like the "plate method," you set yourself up for success. No dramatic diets or cutting food groups here—just smart, steady choices that help keep everything on track.

And for goodness' sake, pay attention to what works for you. We're all different, and our bodies react differently to foods. Pick a strategy that keeps your blood sugar—and **willpower**—steady and strong.

Exercise as a Discipline Booster

You know regular exercise is great for your body, but did you know it's also a **game-changer** for your brain and mood? Exercise gives your **brainpower** a serious boost. When you get moving, your body pumps more blood and oxygen to your brain, helping it work better. It's like tuning up your engine so it runs smoother and faster. Plus, exercise kickstarts the growth of new brain cells. Who wouldn't want that?

Now, let's talk about the **mood** lift. Ever noticed how you feel happier after a workout? That's because exercise releases chemicals called endorphins. These are natural mood lifters, like little happiness bombs going off in your brain. On top of that, exercise reduces stress hormones. So you get less stress and more happiness. It's a win-win!

Setting up a workout plan might sound like a drag, but trust me, it doesn't have to be. Think about what you enjoy. Like swimming? Cool. Prefer running? Awesome. Love dancing? Perfect. Picking something you like makes it way easier to stick with it. Start by jotting down your **goals**. Want to get stronger? Slim down? Feel more energetic? Write it out. That way, you have a clear path.

Once you've got that, create a simple **schedule**. Maybe you start with three days a week. Baby steps are okay. Gradually, as you get more comfortable, add more days or lengthen the sessions. Pro tip: Mix it up. Different workouts keep things fresh and use different muscles. This stops you from getting bored and helps avoid injuries. Variety truly is the spice of life, especially with exercise.

Alright, now for the "habit loop" trick. Making exercise a **habit** takes some smart planning, so it becomes second nature. It all starts with a cue, something that reminds you it's time to move. It could be setting out your workout clothes the night before or having a set time daily. The cue initiates the routine, like hitting play on a video. The routine might be anything from a morning jog to a yoga session. Finish it with a reward. Maybe it's that yummy smoothie or a few moments to relax. The reward gives you something to look forward to, making it that much easier to keep doing.

Here's an extra tip: Pair your workout with something you already love. Love watching TV? Stream your fave show while on the treadmill. Fan of podcasts or audiobooks? Listen while cycling or walking. This way, you blend something you love with something you might not be too keen on.

Setting up your workout:

- Pick activities you enjoy

- Write down your goals

- Make a schedule (start small, build up)

- Diversify your routines

For the habit loop:

- Establish a cue (set workout gear out, stick to the same time)

- Follow with a routine (morning jog, yoga session)

- Conclude with a reward (smoothie, chill time)

Be patient with yourself. It's normal for it to feel tough at the start. The key is **consistency**. Stick it out for a bit and see how your brain gets sharper, your mood brighter, and self-discipline stronger. Before you know it, working out isn't just part of your day. It's part of you. Keep moving—you'll thank yourself later.

Sleep Optimization for Mental Clarity

Getting a good night's **sleep** isn't just about looking fresh or feeling peppy. It's the secret sauce behind rock-solid **decision-making** and self-control. If you're groggy or sleep-deprived, making smart choices throughout the day becomes tougher than you'd think. When you skimp on sleep, your brain's executive function goes a bit haywire, making you more prone to impulsive decisions. It's like trying to drive a car with a foggy windshield. Can you really see what's in front of you? Probably not. Now, extend that foggy vision to your daily tasks and choices, and there you have it—a recipe for bad calls and weak self-control.

So, how do you set yourself up for sleep that's really worth the hours? Creating a solid bedtime **routine** can make all the difference. Ditch those screens an hour before bed. Your phone, tablet, and TV pump out blue light that messes with your body's sleep hormone, melatonin. Instead, grab a book or tune into some chill music. Your body loves rhythm, so try hitting the hay at the same time every night—even on weekends. Think about keeping your room cool and dark. Blackout curtains? Game-changer. Even a slight bump in room temperature can throw your sleep cycles out of whack.

Some teas can help you wind down, like chamomile or lavender. They're soothing and prep your body to relax. But seriously, cut the **caffeine** after noon if you can. It's a sneaky stimulant that could keep you tossing and turning. Speaking of winding down, don't forget about doing something relaxing before bed; it could be a warm bath or some light stretches. The idea is to signal your body that it's time to chill out and get ready for sleep.

Now, let's talk about a technique that works wonders for improving sleep—Progressive Muscle **Relaxation** (PMR). Sounds fancy, but it's straightforward and super effective. PMR involves tensing and then slowly releasing different muscle groups in your body. Focus on one area at a time. Start with your toes, curl and hold them tight for a few seconds before gradually relaxing. Move up to your calves, then thighs, and keep working your way up to your face and even scalp. By focusing on each muscle group and the feeling of letting go, you're shifting your mind away from the day's worries.

Picture your **stress** melting away with each muscle group you release. Your body gets heavier, your heart rate eases up, and your mind starts slowing down—like you're gearing down a car. It's a form of meditation and relaxation rolled into one, helping whisk you off to dreamland.

You'll likely find this PMR routine not just beneficial for falling asleep but for quality sleep, too. It's this kind of deep relaxation that fosters mental **clarity** and helps you wake up ready to face another day of crushing bad habits and resisting temptations.

So, quality sleep and a solid bedtime routine—along with some PMR—can elevate your life in so many ways. Ready to give it a shot? Your body and **mind** will thank you, I promise.

The Mind-Body Connection in Self-Control

Ever felt **stuck** or like you couldn't follow through with your plans? You know, when your mind wants to do one thing but your body seems to ignore the memo? That's where **embodied thinking** comes in. It's the idea that our thoughts aren't just floating in our heads—they're strongly tied to what our bodies are doing.

Take how you sit or stand, for example. Slumping in a chair can make you feel tired or stressed. And when you're slouched over, are you really in prime decision-making mode? Probably not. Sitting up straight, on the other hand, changes everything. You feel more alert, ready to take on whatever comes your way.

Let's think about how you can use **body language** and posture. Because it's not just about looking confident; it's about feeling it too. Trying an open stance can make you braver. Hands on your hips or arms spread out on the desk signals to your brain, "Hey, I got this." And oddly enough, it works.

Feeling indecisive or lacking self-control? Strike a "**power pose**." Imagine a superhero stance. Stand tall, hands on hips, chest out. Research shows that holding this pose for just a couple of minutes can boost **confidence** and even reduce stress. That's not all—you get a nice lift in your self-control too. The trick is convincing your brain that you're powerful, which then makes it easier to act with confidence and control.

It's crazy how this works, but the connection between body and mind is real. When you physically position yourself as a strong, decisive person, your mind goes, "Oh, we're doing this? Ok, let's roll!"

But it's not just a trick to boost your mood. Think about how a boxer bounces before a match, or how marathon runners shake their hands before a race. These actions aren't just habits; they prepare their minds for action. They build a bridge between what they want to think and what their bodies can do.

And minor tweaks to your daily habits can make a world of difference. Simple stuff like:

• Standing tall when waiting for the bus

• Lifting your chin when you walk into a room

• Not folding your arms when having a conversation

These small moves offer subtle yet powerful shifts in your **mindset**.

So, next time you need a little extra boost, remember to check your posture. Feel uncertain before a meeting or a test? Strike that power pose. It's a small act but signals to both your brain and body, "I'm ready, bring it on."

Incorporating this into your routine makes **self-discipline** easier to maintain. So, carry yourself like you mean business and watch as following through with your goals becomes a bit less of a struggle. You aren't just hacking your mind; you're empowering it by commanding your posture.

Our thoughts and actions are intertwined more than we know. What your mind thinks shapes how your body behaves, and vice versa. Strengthen that connection, and you'll find self-discipline becomes less of a chore and more of a natural workflow. It's all connected, and using that can unlock something amazing in your daily grind toward your **goals**.

Practical Exercise: Creating a Holistic Health Plan

Ready to **craft** a health plan that truly works for you? Getting your physical health in check isn't just about shedding those extra pounds or hitting the gym hard. It's a full-body **commitment**. Let's roll up our sleeves and dive in!

First, take stock of your current eating, workout, and sleep habits. It's like taking **inventory**. What are you munching on daily? Think about meals, snacks, even those mindless nibbles. Are they nutrient-packed or more on the junk side? How about your exercise? Whether you're a couch potato or a gym rat, jot it all down. Don't forget about sleep—how many hours are you clocking in, and how consistent are you?

Now, set specific, measurable **goals** for each part of your physical health. Get real with yourself. What do you want to fix? Maybe you're aiming to eat more fruits and veggies, hit the gym more often, or finally snag those elusive eight hours of shut-eye. Make sure your goals are crystal clear and doable. Instead of a vague "I'll eat healthier," go for something like "I'll gobble up five servings of fruits and veggies every day."

Next, whip up a weekly meal plan that supports your nutrition goals. Let's map out a menu. Start simple. Maybe a smoothie for breakfast, a balanced salad for lunch, and lean protein for dinner. Don't forget snacks—think nuts, fruits, or veggies with hummus. Once you've got a basic plan, you can get fancy with recipes.

Time to plan a workout **routine** that fits your schedule and preferences. This isn't about going all-out from day one. Choose a routine that seems manageable and fun. If mornings aren't your jam, maybe evenings work better. Mix it up with cardio, strength training, and some yoga or stretching. The key is finding what you enjoy, so it doesn't feel like a chore.

Stick to a consistent sleep schedule and bedtime routine. Good sleep starts with a pattern. Try setting a sleep and wake time, even on weekends. Develop a bedtime ritual—maybe some light reading, a warm bath, or meditation. Staying away from screens an hour before bed really helps too.

Now, follow your plan for two weeks, keeping **track** of your progress every day. Here's where the rubber meets the road. Put your plan into action and note how it goes. Meal logs, workout checklists, and sleep diaries can make it easier. It helps you stay accountable and see where you could make some tweaks.

Pay attention to how it affects your energy, focus, and self-discipline. Notice any changes in how you feel. More pep in your step? Feeling less sluggish? Take mental notes, or even real ones. Your body's responses can clue you in on how well things are working.

Finally, **tweak** your plan based on what you find and keep going for another month. If something's not quite clicking, make some adjustments. Maybe you need more variety in your meals, or perhaps you're exercising too much and need a break day. Adapt the plan to better suit your needs and continue on for another month.

By getting a handle on your physical health, you'll see improvements in energy, focus, and even your willpower. You've got this plan laid out—just keep refining it as you go, making note of what does and doesn't work for you. This isn't about overnight muscles or drastic results. It's about slow, steady improvements, shaping your habits, and ultimately helping you reach those bigger goals in life.

In Conclusion

Great physical **health** doesn't just make your body strong; it sharpens your mind and boosts self-discipline. This chapter showed how proper **nutrition**, regular **exercise**, and quality **sleep** can help you stay focused and make better decisions.

You've seen some cool ways nutrition can help your brain and body stay **energized**. You've learned about exercises that don't feel like chores but make you happier and more focused. Sleep can be your secret weapon for staying sharp and in control. You've discovered special tricks for using your body to boost your mental **power**. Plus, you've picked up tips for creating an all-in-one health plan that fits your life perfectly.

When you eat well, move around, and sleep enough, everything seems easier, right? Keep these ideas in mind, and you can use them every day for a healthier, happier, and more disciplined **life**. The **effort** you put in today will make you stronger and more resilient tomorrow. You have the power to shape your future one small habit at a time, so get started and keep going!

Chapter 10: Emotional Regulation and Self-Discipline

Ever wonder why some folks keep their cool while others seem to explode at the slightest problem? I used to be the latter—quick to anger, slow to calm down. But you don't have to navigate life on an emotional rollercoaster. In this chapter, we'll explore how you can transform emotional **chaos** into clarity and purpose.

Imagine **smashing** through the roadblocks of emotional outbursts and impulsive reactions—one step at a time. Here, you'll find the tools to identify and manage those pesky emotional **triggers**. I asked myself countless times, "Why can't I control my feelings?" You're not alone here. Together, we'll pick up some practical **techniques** for emotional self-control.

Think about using emotions like gas in a car; they can drive **motivation** or lead to burnout. You'll learn how to channel emotions as fuel for your daily grind rather than letting them steer you off course.

Developing emotional **intelligence** is your secret weapon. Ever had a conversation where the other person just gets you? That could be you, mastering the art of understanding and responding to emotions—yours and others'.

To wrap it up, we'll do some hands-on **exercises** in emotion tracking and response planning. Sound too good to be true? Well, give it a shot, and see how your everyday life starts to feel a bit more manageable and a lot more **fulfilling**. So, are you ready to take control of your emotional world?

Identifying and Managing Emotional Triggers

Let's talk about **emotional smarts**. Some folks call it Emotional Intelligence, but emotional smarts just seems to capture it better. So, what does it mean? Basically, it's understanding your own emotions and the emotions of others. It helps you stay aware, so you don't go off the handle every time something doesn't go your way.

Think of it this way, if you've got emotional smarts, you're like a **surfer** who knows how to ride every wave, no matter how big or small. You know when your temper's rising, and you can keep yourself from snapping.

How do you get better at this? Start by keeping a **log**. Yup, just grab a notebook or an app. What sets you off? Write it down. Maybe it's your boss bouncing in with last-minute work. Or, when someone cuts you off in traffic. Keep track of who, what, and when. You'll start seeing patterns.

For example:

• Mondays are rough. Is it because you stayed up too late on Sunday night?

• Your friend Charles always gets under your skin with his bragging. Every. Single. Time.

• Speaking of traffic, any delay over 5 minutes and you're fuming.

Spot the patterns, and you'll have a better idea of what's **triggering** you. It's like mapping out the minefield before you walk through it.

Once you know your triggers, you've got to do something about them. One trick that really helps? The **STOP** method. It's a lifesaver. This is how it works:

Stop. Literally just stop whatever you're doing. Freeze. Don't react immediately.

Take a breath. Deep breaths. Inhale, exhale. Slows you down, calms you a bit.

Observe. What exactly are you feeling? Anger, frustration, envy? Notice what's going on. What are you thinking? Is your heart racing?

Proceed. Move forward, but with intention. Decide what to do next, based on what you've just figured out about your emotions.

Let's break that down with an example.

Imagine your partner says something that immediately gets on your nerves. Usually, your gut reaction is a snappy comeback. But this time, you STOP. You breathe in deeply for a moment to collect yourself. Your mind's a bit clearer now, and you start to OBSERVE. What are you actually feeling? Maybe it's not really anger but hurt. They've touched a sensitive spot without realizing.

Now you can PROCEED. You can choose to close the subject nicely: "Hey, can we talk about this later? I need a bit of time to think." Could be a tougher **discussion**, but it'll go smoother when you're not riding a wave of fury.

Life's full of these trigger moments. Keeping an eye on them, and using methods like STOP, helps you handle those strong feelings. You won't always get it perfect, and that's okay. **Progress** is what counts. And your emotional smarts improve each time you practice.

Techniques for Emotional Self-Control

Feeling things deeply? You're not alone. **Emotions** can guide you, drive you, and sometimes mess you up. Let's talk about managing those feelings and not letting them run the show.

First off, having a good **vocabulary** for your feelings is like having a well-stocked toolbox. Imagine needing to fix something but only having a hammer. Frustrating, right? Same with emotions. If all you can say is "I'm sad" or "I'm angry," you're missing out on nuance. Maybe you're not just sad; maybe you're feeling lonely, disappointed, or even nostalgic. Knowing those words can boost your self-awareness, making it easier to figure out what's really going on with you.

For example, say you're feeling super stressed. Maybe you're actually feeling **overwhelmed** because you have too much on your plate. Or maybe you're anxious because you have an upcoming deadline. Different feelings, different solutions. Words help...a lot! So grab a list of feeling words and start using them. The more you name it, the easier it is to tame it.

Next, let's tackle **cognitive reframing**—basically changing how you see a situation to feel differently about it. Stuff happens. Life's tough. But you can flip the script. Think of that ultra-annoying coworker. Instead of seeing him as a walking headache, consider this: maybe he's great at seeing things you miss. Instead of "Annoying Tom who criticizes everything," he becomes "Observant Tom who catches details." Your feelings about him change because you've changed how you look at him.

This works in all sorts of situations. Having a rough day at work? Yeah, it sucks. But maybe it's a good lesson in resilience. Didn't get the job you wanted? Sure, disappointing. But maybe it's a reroute to something even better. See where I'm going with this? It's not just positive thinking; it's smart thinking.

Alright, let's drop some knowledge on "**emotional distancing**." This is basically stepping back from your emotions to get a clearer view of what's really happening. Think of your emotions as a storm. When you're in the middle of it, all you get is rain and wind. But if you could rise above the storm and look down, you'd see the bigger picture.

Here's a trick to try. Next time you're super angry or really sad, ask yourself, "How would I advise a friend in this situation?" Or, "What will I think about this in a year?" Creating that distance helps you respond more logically rather than reacting impulsively. Suddenly, the overwhelming feeling shrinks. Your anger might turn into just mild annoyance, or your sadness into something more manageable.

Okay, so we've talked about naming your emotions, seeing things differently, and stepping back from your intense feelings. But weaving these together makes **emotional self-control** even stronger. You observe your mood swings, rethink your rough patches, and create some breathing room when things are intense. Practice this combo regularly—especially when stuff hits the fan—and you'll see a noticeable change in your **self-discipline**.

Nobody nails this stuff overnight. Me? Still a work in progress. Keep at it, though, and you'll find it starts to come naturally. Pretty soon, you'll manage your **emotions**, not the other way around. Handy trick, no?

Using Emotions as Motivation

When it comes to **motivating** yourself, emotions can be your secret weapon. Don't shy away from either the good or the bad. It's all about harnessing what you're feeling and turning it into fuel for your actions and goals.

Let's say you're feeling super happy about something. Maybe you landed that job you wanted or you finally managed to get up early and go for a run. Use that positive vibe to keep pushing yourself. When you're happy, you're more likely to feel energized and ready to tackle new challenges. Make happiness an anchor—a reminder of the rewards of sticking with your goals.

But hey, what if you're in a bad mood? Maybe you're frustrated or feeling down because things aren't going your way. Don't just wallow in it. Anger and frustration can also drive you to make changes. Channel that feeling to smash through obstacles. Use it as a motivation to say, "Okay, I'm tired of things being this way. It's time for a change."

Creating emotional **anchors** can be a game-changer for your disciplined choices, too. Imagine these anchors as mental bookmarks. Every time something makes you feel good or bad about a decision, bookmark that emotional state. For example, let's say you hit the gym and feel pumped afterward. Keep that feeling handy. Next time you're tempted to skip the gym, pull up that bookmark. Remind yourself of how great you'll feel afterward.

It works the other way too. Say you gave into the temptation and binged on junk food. Bookmark that sluggish, guilty feeling. When you're facing that bag of chips again, recall that yucky post-binge experience. It'll make resisting the temptation a bit easier.

Now, let's talk about the "future self" **visualization** method. This one is pretty fun, actually. Think of it as play-acting for your brain. Picture yourself down the road. How do you want to feel? What do you want to have achieved? Get really detailed with it. Imagine waking up, feeling like a success. You nail all your goals. You're happy. You're thriving. Picture the small details, like the smile on your face when you reach a long-standing goal or the sense of peace uncluttering your life gives you.

When you have a clear image of your future self, use it to **motivate** your current self. Whenever you're tempted to skip the tougher choices, bring that future self to mind. It'll help you realize that every disciplined action you take right now is a step toward becoming that person. It bridges the gap between who you are and who you want to be, making it a little easier to stick with your plans.

Making this a **habit** requires a bit of practice. It might feel weird at first to give your feelings so much credit. But over time, linking your disciplined actions with both your emotions and your future self's will make the process feel more natural. You'll start to respond to emotions as signals rather than distractions, using them to stay motivated and focused.

In essence, **emotions** don't just have to control you. You can harness them, anchor them, and project them into the future. It's a powerful way to bolster your **self-discipline**, without constantly fighting against your feelings. So, whenever you're in doubt or struggling to keep going, just tap into those emotions. They'll guide you—maybe not in perfectly straight lines, but in a direction that feels aligned with your truest **goals**.

Developing Emotional Intelligence

Let's chat about **emotional** smarts. Being emotionally smart involves four things: knowing yourself, managing yourself, understanding others, and handling relationships. Master these, and you're golden.

First up is knowing yourself. This means figuring out what you're **feeling** and why. When you understand your own emotions, it's easier to manage them. Try this neat trick: name your feelings.

Sounds basic, right? But saying, "I'm stressed" or "I'm excited" helps you get a grip on what's going on inside. It's like shining a light on those dark corners of your mind. Want to go deeper? Keep a feelings journal. Jot down how you feel throughout the day. Patterns might pop up – maybe Tuesday mornings suck because of that weekly meeting. When you know this, you can do something about it.

Next, let's talk about managing yourself. Yeah, it's not always easy. Emotions can be like wild horses. But you learn to ride them, not let them run wild. Simple tactics help. Deep breaths, a short walk, or even just counting to ten. Little things that make a big difference. I always find that a quick breather rewires my brain, gives me pause before I react. Practice **patience**. Don't think of it as waiting—it's more about pacing yourself, so you don't explode or make hasty decisions.

Now, understanding others. This is where **empathy** kicks in. It's like stepping into someone else's shoes. To do this, you've got to really listen. Not just hear words, but get where the other person's coming from. Eye contact helps—makes it clear you're focused and care. Nodding along or saying, "I get it," goes a long way. This builds trust and rapport. And that's huge. Look for social cues, too. If someone's folding their arms, maybe they're closed off. If they're leaning in, they're engaged. Reading body language can be a real eye-opener.

And now we're at handling **relationships**. People skills, essentially. Be mindful about how you communicate. Clear, calm, and thoughtful responses over impulsive, dramatic ones. Sort of like tuning an old-school radio—find that sweet spot so you're not too loud or too silent. Conflicts happen, but it's about resolving them without burning bridges. Apologize when needed. Own your mistakes. Asking, "How can we fix this together?" rather than pointing fingers makes all the difference. This kind of humility and openness wins people over.

In a nutshell, emotional smarts are a skill worth acing. They can turn tricky situations into easier ones. You've got knowing yourself down—great job naming those feelings. You've learned ways to manage yourself better—deep breaths and patience are on your side. Understanding others and handling relationships wrap it up, rounding out your emotional smartness **journey**.

Using these tips, facing bad habits and temptations gets easier. More control over emotions means less self-sabotage. You'll crush those **goals**—trust the process. Hey, emotional smarts is no walk in the park, but you're on your way. Wishing you all the **success** in the world!

Practical Exercise: Emotion Tracking and Response Planning

Let's dive into tackling **emotional regulation** through an easy-to-understand exercise. This will really help you out. It all starts with keeping an **emotion log**. Just grab a notebook or use your phone for this. Over the course of a week, jot down your emotional experiences daily. And we're not talking just the big stuff. Note moments when you feel stressed, happy, angry, etc. You know, all the feelings.

After you've filled your log for a week, flip through those pages and see if you can spot some **patterns**. Are there specific **triggers** for certain emotions? It could be traffic, a person, or a workload. And how do you react to these feelings? Maybe you lash out when you're angry or reach for junk food when stressed. Finding these patterns is key to understanding yourself better.

Next up, pick three common emotional challenges from those patterns. Maybe it's your reaction to criticism, stress at work, or arguments at home. Choose the ones that pop up the most. These will be your focus areas.

Now, let's come up with a specific **plan** for handling each challenge. For instance, if criticism makes you angry, plan to take a deep breath and count to ten before responding. Or if work stress is getting to you, maybe a 5-minute walk every hour could help. The idea is to have a set game plan for those tough moments.

When you get triggered, put your plans to the test. Keep your emotion log handy and note down what triggered you, what your plan was, and how well you could stick to it. Maybe you'll ace it or maybe you won't. It's all part of the process.

Every day, think about how your **strategies** worked out. Did deep breathing help when you got that harsh feedback? If not, what might work better? It's all about tweaking and adjusting. If one plan doesn't work, try modifying it. Maybe a quick chat with a friend would have been more effective than a walk.

Stick with it for a month. Yeah, it might feel like a lot, but this practice is like a skill. The more you do it, the better you become. Your emotional regulation muscles, so to speak, get stronger over time. This practice can really help in growing your emotional regulation skills. And honestly, it'll make you feel a lot more in control, which is great for your **self-discipline** journey.

Keep checking in with your log and reassessing those plans. By the end of the month, you'll probably find that you're better at handling those same old triggers. Maybe you won't feel as stressed, or you'll have a better strategy for dealing with rude comments.

This exercise is a practical way to take charge of your emotions and reactions. So, keep jotting down, spotting those patterns, testing your plans, and tweaking them. Before you know it, you'll notice significant **improvement** in how you manage your emotions, making you more disciplined day by day.

Got any thoughts or stories to share? Taking time to think about what's working and what isn't definitely makes a difference. This whole thing isn't about being perfect; it's about progressing each day. Stick with it, reflect often, and watch as you become more emotionally resilient and disciplined.

Hope you're feeling excited to put this into action. Let's go!

Conclusion

This chapter has taken you on a journey to understand the crucial **connection** between your emotions and self-discipline. You've learned the keys to identifying emotional triggers, using emotions to **motivate** yourself, and increasing your emotional intelligence. By mastering these skills, you can better manage yourself and reach your **goals** despite challenges.

You've seen how the concept of emotional intelligence matters for self-discipline. You've learned about creating an emotional trigger log to spot patterns in your feelings. The "STOP" technique can help you calm intense emotions and take smart actions. You've discovered the importance of building a strong emotional **vocabulary** to boost self-awareness. Plus, you now know how to use both happy and tough emotions as fuel to drive your goals.

This chapter offers practical **tools** and insights that can lead to better self-control and motivation. By applying what you've learned, you can turn emotions into a powerful **ally** rather than letting them control you. Embrace these strategies, keep practicing, and watch as your self-discipline grows stronger every day. Your emotions are here to **guide** you; learn to navigate them well, and take confident steps toward achieving your goals!

I hope you'll take these ideas to heart and put them into action. Remember, your emotions can be your greatest **asset** when you learn to work with them. So go ahead, embrace your feelings, and let them propel you towards success!

Chapter 11: Productivity Techniques for the Disciplined Mind

Ever felt like you're juggling too many tasks at once? You're not alone. You might think you're being **productive** by handling everything simultaneously, but are you really? There's a whole different approach you could take, one where you reclaim your time and keep your sanity. As you dive into this chapter, you'll discover how shifting your **focus** can completely transform your day.

Imagine you're faced with dozens of small tasks. BAM! The Two-Minute Rule turns them into quick wins! Meanwhile, finding the magic in **batching** similar stuff makes you more effective than ever before. How, you ask? Just wait till you give it a shot.

But you're probably wondering: isn't technology the biggest time-eater? Well, it can also be your best friend if you know how to use it smartly. You'll pick up tricks with **productivity** apps that change your workflow, just like flipping a switch. Lastly, real **progress** happens with practical exercises, right? This chapter wraps up with you doing a productivity check-up. Real actions, real results.

So, buckle up and get ready. By the time you finish this chapter, you won't be just another busy person. You're poised to **master** that to-do list and become a **productivity** powerhouse. Your **disciplined** mind is about to take center stage, transforming how you tackle tasks and manage your time. Get ready to unlock your full potential and become the efficiency guru you've always wanted to be.

Single-Tasking vs. Multitasking

Everyone thinks they're a great **multitasker** these days. But let's talk about the cost of bouncing between tasks and how it messes with your **productivity**. Spoiler: it's not good.

Switching between tasks isn't as smooth as you might think. Your **brain** takes time to adjust to new contexts, and this switching sucks up mental energy. Imagine trying to read a book and having to stop every few pages to watch TV. You wouldn't really get into the book, right? It's the same deal with multitasking. When you switch tasks, your brain has to re-focus, and while it does that, you're losing precious moments. In fact, some studies say it can take up to 23 minutes to refocus fully. Crazy, huh?

The mental costs also pile up in other ways. Each time you shift gears, you're using bits and pieces of your cognitive resources, like willpower and attention span. Think of it as having a limited amount of "brain currency" to spend each day. Spending it on task-switching leaves less for the actual **work** you need to finish. It's like trying to run errands in multiple places at once, always scattering your effort.

So, how do you fix this? Well, setting up a good **workspace** is a game-changer here. Make it a place where you can dive into one thing at a time. Reduce clutter. Your workspace should only have what you need for your current task. No extra papers, sticky notes, or gadgets that could snag your attention.

Start by choosing your "focus zone." Pick a spot where distractions are minimal. If you can dedicate an area just for work or for a specific type of task, that's even better. Leave your phone and other distracting gadgets in another room. Try facing away from doorways or busy areas. This makes it easier to keep your brain locked in on the job at hand.

Lighting and seating matter, too. Natural light can do wonders for your **focus**, so set up near a window if you can. A comfy chair isn't just about being seated but about fostering a space where you feel ready to tackle tasks for extended periods.

Got a structure? Good. Let's move to one of the nifty tricks—task **batching**. It's about grouping similar tasks and knocking them out in one go. Think about when you do laundry. It's a bunch easier to wash, dry, and fold clothes all in one shot rather than spreading it out over the week. Apply that logic to work.

Task batching can make a big difference. For example, handle all your emails at once instead of checking them constantly. Schedule all your calls back-to-back. Doing so keeps you in the same frame of mind, making transitions smoother and quicker.

Consider using apps or planners to see these batches visually. Write down tasks you often repeat, then plan them into your day as blocks. The idea here is to create a chunk of time dedicated to a specific type of activity. It's like setting up mini-projects you can completely focus on without interruptions.

Now, there's nothing magical going to come out of nowhere and fix everything—you've got to consciously make these changes. It's like a muscle you need to train. The more you practice single-tasking and batching, the more natural it'll feel, and the better you'll get at **focusing**.

That's everything for single-tasking vs. multitasking, in a casual, get-it-done tone. Once you really feel the benefits, sticking to it won't feel like work—it'll just make sense.

The Two-Minute Rule for Small Tasks

You know that satisfying feeling when you check stuff off your to-do list? Feels amazing, right? Well, that's what the Two-Minute

Rule is all about. When you can **accomplish** tasks quickly, it's like giving your brain a little hit of happiness. You're basically saying, "Look at me! Getting stuff done!" And guess what? This little trick doesn't just make you feel good, it also preps you to tackle bigger challenges.

Let's find those tiny tasks you're gonna crush in no time. Start by taking a peek at your to-do list. Got a bunch of little things? Good news—they're perfect for this. Things like replying to an email, sending a quick text, or filing away that one piece of paper—these are prime candidates. Sometimes you just need to use this rule—for example, if something seems like it'll take forever, it probably doesn't qualify. But when you spot stuff you know you can handle quickly, you're on the right **track**.

"Do it now" is a **mantra** you should live by. Seriously, it stops all those little things from piling up and turning into one big headache. Think of it like dealing with dirty dishes—don't let them sit around or soon you'll have a sink full of gross stuff. So, you see that email sitting there? Respond to it. Is there trash on the floor? Pick it up. These small actions might feel insignificant, but they make a massive difference in keeping your space, whether mental or physical, clear and ready.

Here's an example: let's say you're at work and your boss asks for a quick update. Instead of putting it off 'cause you think you need more time, realize it takes two minutes. If you don't, that quick update turns into stress five minutes later when they ask again. Get it done now and move on. So easy.

Why do small tasks matter so much? Well, they clear mental **clutter**. Look, your brain is like your phone—too many open apps slow everything down. Close these mental apps by dealing with them fast. Every time you handle a task quickly, that's one less thing weighing you down. It'll keep you feeling light and **productive**.

Let's chat about spotting tiny tasks. You could develop a little routine for this. Every morning, scan your to-do list. Stuff you can handle in a snap gets marked. By the afternoon, those are usually done. Another method is setting a mental timer when approaching tasks. If it can be tackled in the span of a TV commercial, it's a quick win.

Worried about letting small stuff pile up? Use this trick: when you can do it immediately, do it. Develop a **habit**, and it slowly becomes a reflex. Before you know it, your workload magically seems lighter. That's because you've tackled those dime-sized chores instead of letting them chill until they become a dollar.

Finding small tasks isn't just about items on your list now. Look around your life—like spots or activities—where stuff can be done quickly. Whether at home, work, or between activities, there're always small bits you can handle.

To wrap things up, the Two-Minute Rule isn't just about small tasks—it's a fundamental part of becoming more productive. It's your **strategy** to keep tiny chores from becoming tomorrow's monsters. Spot them, sort them, and tackle them quickly. You'll realize that knocking out even the tiniest tasks has a BIG impact on your productivity. Yeah, the phrase might sound like self-help lingo, but in truth, it's incredibly **practical**. Give it a shot, you won't regret it.

Batching Similar Activities

Switching between tasks all the time really **drains** your mental energy. That's what's called context switching. Imagine you're reading a book, and someone interrupts you every five minutes to talk about something unrelated. You'd lose your train of thought and constantly have to find your place again. That's what your brain goes through each time you switch from one task to another. It takes extra effort to refocus, which weighs you down mentally.

It's so much smoother if you group similar tasks together. Think about all those little tasks you do every day. Answering emails, making phone calls, doing admin work. If you bounce between these and something totally unrelated, you're draining your brain power faster. When you put similar activities together, your brain stays in a similar mode. Less transition time.

Here's what can help you stay **organized**: themed days. It's where you dedicate specific days to specific tasks or categories. Mondays could be for meetings and planning your week's work. Tuesdays might be for creative stuff—designing or writing. Maybe Wednesdays are for client work or customer service. I've tried this trick, and it really does make things less chaotic and more manageable.

Organizing your life this way doesn't just reduce **stress**, it also boosts your **productivity**. You get into a groove with whatever type of work you're doing. Say you've planned all your content for your website or social media on Thursdays. Your brain's in "content creation mode". Switching in and out of it means you're less efficient. Sticking with it for a time improves your workflow. Besides, it feels good to check off a whole set of related tasks.

Making it even simpler—think of it like you're wearing different hats on different days. Monday's hat could be your 'strategic planner' hat. Tuesday, 'creator' hat. When it's time for one hat, all your mental gears shift to fit that role. This way your brain isn't jumping from one type of task to another all the time. You'll feel more in control. It's like autopilot for efficiency.

Be real though, life happens. Maybe you planned Thursday as your 'deep work' day. Stuff pops up, distractions come knocking. Flexible doesn't mean ditching the plan, just bending it a bit. Sometimes moving chunks of work around helps. Today wasn't great for meetings? Shift that themed day to a less hectic one. Got a meeting-free day next week? Might be that ideal deep focus day you need.

This isn't about rigid rules, it's more about creating a **routine** that keeps you sane and productive. For instance, block out time in your calendar for similar tasks. Keep that block sacred unless there's an urgent thing. Each time you save yourself from context switching, your brain thanks you. Boost your capacity to actually finish tasks instead of always starting new ones.

To sum it up, working in **batches** and having themed days sounds basic but packs a punch. Less stress, more done. Following this approach gives you clearer **focus** without burning out. Give your brain a break from the constant shifting. Streamline and batch those tasks. You'll feel much more **organized**—and way more efficient.

Using Technology to Enhance Productivity

Ever feel like your digital life needs a bit of a cleanup? That's where **digital minimalism** steps in. It's all about keeping your tech use to the bare essentials. You rely on gadgets and apps, but having too many can be super distracting. Think of it like having a tidy desk—it keeps you focused on what really matters.

So, what's the trick here? Use only the **tools** that actually help you get stuff done. Turn off unnecessary notifications. Keep just the apps you'd use daily. Only follow really useful social media accounts. That way, you cut out the clutter and boost your focus.

But, with so many options, how do you pick the right **productivity apps**? Everyone works differently, so start by figuring out your work style. Are you a list-maker? Try apps like Todoist or Microsoft To-Do. Think visually? Maybe Trello or Asana suits you better. Or perhaps you prefer simple timers like Focus Booster. Test out a few to see which feels the best. Don't force yourself to use an app just because it's popular.

Also, don't overload your device with too many apps. That's kind of the opposite of what you're aiming for. Stick to the basics, and make sure they actually help you accomplish things, not confuse you with endless features.

Speaking of keeping things tidy, ever hear of a "**tech audit**"? It's like a spring cleaning for your digital world. Once in a while, go through your devices and ditch what you don't need. Outdated apps, random downloads, and unused browser extensions can all go. It's surprisingly freeing.

How do you do it? Start with your apps. Open each one and see if you still use it. No? Delete it. Check your downloads folder and clear out the clutter. On your phone, do the same. Less is more here. The fewer **distractions** you have, the more you can get done.

Once you've cleaned up, think about how to keep things streamlined. Maybe set a reminder to do a mini tech audit every couple of months. That way, your devices stay clean and handy.

So there you go—use digital minimalism to keep your **focus** sharp. Pick productivity apps that suit your style and actually help you. And finally, tidy up your tech with a thorough tech audit. These small steps can make a big difference in staying **productive** and disciplined.

Phew, that wasn't so bad, was it? Now, back to work with a cleared mind and an uncluttered device. Easy, right?

Practical Exercise: Productivity Audit and Improvement Plan

Ready to take a good, honest look at your **productivity** levels? Buckle up, it's gonna be a bit of work. For the next seven days, jot down what you do, how long each task takes, and how productive you feel during each activity. We're talking about everything here. From the minute you start your day till you hit the sack. Keep it real—both the wins and the time you spend scrolling through social media. By the end of the week, you'll see some patterns forming.

Mulling over your data, think about when you're super **productive**. Those golden hours when you're in the zone—write those times down. Also, point out your biggest **distractions**. That could be your phone, noisy roommates, or even hunger pangs. Identifying both helps spot where changes are needed. It's like figuring out your very own rhythm.

Next, consider what you're using to keep on track. Note down any methods and **tools** you use to stay productive. This can be a to-do list on your phone, Post-it notes everywhere, or that productivity app everyone's raving about. Lay it all bare. Also, how effective do you find these tools? You've gotta be honest. If your app is making tasks feel like a chore, it's probably not working. Maybe that colorful planner is mostly gathering dust. This audit will give you a clearer picture.

But hey, keep an open mind. Look up other productivity **hacks** and tricks online or ask friends what they swear by. Finding fresh tactics can be a game changer. Now, pick a new trick to try each week for a month. This is vital—don't try all at once. You want to see a genuine impact, not just chaos.

Each week, as you try a new trick, write down what happens. How did you feel? Did you get more done, feel more relaxed, or was it another dud? These notes will be golden. They paint a clearer picture of what actually helps and what's just hype.

Having compiled all that wisdom over a month's span, it's time to blend it all into a custom **productivity** plan. Draw from the successful tricks and ditch the useless ones. Create a **routine** based on when you're most productive, minimizing distractions you've already identified. It's your perfect mix—tailored precisely to you!

But don't forget, you're never locked into one thing. Circumstances change, work pressure fluctuates, so give yourself room for tweaks. **Flexibility** could be your best friend here.

So, what's the takeaway? Focus—Really track your week. Find the productive moments and those pesky distractions. List down what you're using to stay on top—and judge them honestly. Hunt for new tricks. Give each a week. Write out your experience. Then, craft a tailored productivity plan. It's all about fine-tuning what works for YOU. Keeping it dynamic and responsive is key. You've got all the tools you need. All set?

In Conclusion

This chapter has unveiled some **crucial secrets** to boosting your productivity. It's all about **focusing** on one task at a time, managing small chores quickly, grouping similar activities, using tech tools wisely, and auditing your productivity habits. Each of these tips is a way for you to become more **efficient** and get things done more smoothly. Just imagine how much you'll **accomplish** by incorporating these techniques into your daily life!

You've learned about single-tasking versus multitasking and why it's better to zero in on one thing instead of juggling many. The two-minute rule for small tasks has shown you the perks of handling quick chores right away. You've also discovered how **batching** similar activities can save you time and energy.

When it comes to technology, you've seen the best ways to use digital tools without falling into the **distraction** trap. The practical exercise on productivity audit and improvement has given you a step-by-step guide to track and boost your efficiency.

By putting these methods to work, you'll handle tasks more effectively and stay on top of things. Give these tips a shot, and you'll be amazed at how much more you can **achieve** day by day. Try them out and enjoy the sense of **accomplishment** that comes with ramping up your productivity!

So, what are you waiting for? It's time to put these **strategies** into action and watch your productivity soar!

Chapter 12: Overcoming Procrastination

Have you ever sat there, staring at a task, and thought, "I'll just do it later"? Yeah, we've all been there. But what if I told you that **procrastination** is more than just a bad habit? It's like this sneaky thief that steals your time and energy, right under your nose.

In this chapter, we're going to get to the **root** of why you procrastinate. It feels like a detective story, doesn't it? You're going to uncover clues about yourself you didn't even know existed. Ever heard of "eating that frog"? It's this technique you'd never think to try, but trust me, it'll change your whole game in getting stuff done.

Don't worry, I won't ask you to climb mountains or anything. We'll work on breaking things down into **bite-sized** tasks. Imagine transforming that big, scary **project** into bits you can handle without breaking a sweat. Pretty handy, right?

As you read on, you'll learn about some cool tricks to hold yourself **accountable**. You know, so things actually get done. And for the hands-on folks, there's a neat **challenge** crafted just for busting procrastination—think of it as a fun test to see your progress.

Ready? Let's get that pesky **procrastination** handled once and for all. By the time you're done with this chapter, you'll have the **tools** to tackle your to-do list like a pro. No more putting things off until tomorrow. It's time to seize the day and make procrastination a thing of the past!

Root Causes of Procrastination

Ever wondered why you **procrastinate**? It's a question that nags at you from time to time. It all starts in your mind. There's a lot going on up there, and some of it doesn't exactly help you get things done. Let's break it down a bit.

One big reason is **fear**. You're scared you won't do a good job or that you'll fail. So, you dodge the task, thinking, "I'll do it tomorrow." Guess what? Tomorrow never comes. Sometimes, you might even fear success. Sounds weird, right? But achieving something can bring new responsibilities and expectations. That can feel pretty daunting too.

Another culprit? You might think perfect is the only way to go. **Perfectionism** makes you believe if you can't do it flawlessly, don't do it at all. This makes tasks seem huge and intimidating. So, you put them off.

Or maybe, you're just not into the task. Lack of **interest** or excitement can push you to put things off. When something feels boring or unimportant, it's easy to say, "I'll get to it later."

And let's not forget about **uncertainty**. Not knowing where to begin or what the steps are can make the whole thing seem overwhelming. When you don't know how to start, not starting at all seems like a safer bet.

So, how can you spot your own triggers and habits? It's kind of like playing detective on yourself. Start looking at when you procrastinate. Is it with work, study, cleaning, or something else? Do you procrastinate more in the mornings or evenings?

Watch what you do when you're dragging your feet. Do you find yourself scrolling through social media, binging on shows, or something else? That's a clue. Your procrastination tells a story about what's holding you back.

Once you know the triggers, you can work on them. Let's say you notice you put off tasks that feel too big. Spotting that can help you break the task into smaller, more manageable pieces. **Chunking** makes it less scary and can get you moving.

Have you ever heard of the "5 Whys" method? It's a cool way to dig deep into why you procrastinate. Here's how it works. Start by asking why you're putting something off. For instance, if you say, "I keep avoiding starting that report," ask yourself why. Maybe you answer, "I'm afraid I'll mess it up." Then ask again, "Why am I afraid I'll mess it up?" Continue this until you've asked why five times. By the fifth why, you often uncover the root cause.

For example:

• Why am I not starting the report? Because I feel like it's too difficult.

• Why do I feel like it's too difficult? Because I have never done anything like this before.

• Why haven't I done anything like this before? Because new tasks make me nervous.

• Why do new tasks make me nervous? Because I fear I won't be good at them.

• Why do I fear I won't be good? Because I'm afraid of failure.

So, what you're really dealing with is a fear of failing. Understanding this can help you take steps to tackle that fear, rather than just avoiding the task.

In a nutshell, overcoming **procrastination** is a mental game. It's about understanding what's going on in your head and recognizing your own triggers. And when you get to the bottom of why you put things off, you can find ways to fix those reasons. No more dilly-dallying, it's about moving forward.

The "Eat That Frog" Technique

Ever look at your to-do list and feel like **avoiding** the biggest task? Yeah, I do too. It's a huge temptation. That's where the "Eat That Frog" technique comes in handy. The idea's simple—**tackle** the toughest, most important task first. Just like eating a frog, you get the worst part out of the way, freeing you to glide through the rest of your tasks. Sounds pretty good, right?

It's really all about **momentum**. You get that big, ugly task done first thing in the morning, and it sets the tone for a productive day. Plus, you don't spend the whole day dreading and procrastinating. When you've conquered the mountain, everything else is just a small hill. The good news? You'll get used to it. And once that happens, putting it off won't be your default anymore. Cool, huh?

But how do you spot which task is the 'frog'? Look at your list and pick the one that's either the hardest or the most impactful—or often, both. Time-consuming project. Important report. That phone call you've been putting off. Anything that demands lots of attention and gives you those stress butterflies just thinking about it.

Ranking the frogs in the pond is your next move. Make a short list of tasks you've got to do that day—rank 'em from most **challenging** or important, down to the simple stuff. Your top few items are your frogs. This leaves room for quick wins while keeping your gaze on the ultimate prize.

And here's another trick: time **blocking**. It means setting sections of your day aside just for those tough tasks. Carving out 1-2 hour blocks means nothing else gets a look-in during that time. Your phone? MIA. Your inbox? Ignored. Keeping interruptions out and focus in helps make good progress. It's like putting up a "Do Not Disturb" sign for your brain.

Start small. Don't think you need a four-hour marathon on the first go. Try focusing for a manageable stretch, like 30 minutes to an hour. From here it's an easy expand into longer blocks. More focused time on frog tasks can limit endless efforting later.

Feeling isolated? Make a pact with a buddy—prodding each other to stay on task. **Productivity's** often easier with someone plugged in. Being a lone wolf isn't always the best approach.

Once it's all set, brace yourself before diving into your saved rationed blocks. Come morning, eat your first (meaningful) frog with a hearty dose of **dedication**. Most pain minimization lies in early execution. Putting it off might only make things harder.

Is one frog squeezed in? You'll quickly notice a sense of **accomplishment** washing over you. Keep cultivating this 'frog-eating' habit and you might even inspire others to follow suit. Before you know it, you'll be the reigning master of efficiency!

And here's the kicker... As you keep at it, you'll find yourself tackling tasks you never thought possible. Your newfound momentum will have you soaring to new heights, conquering challenges left and right. It's like unlocking a whole new level of productivity, where even the toughest tasks become manageable stepping stones to success.

Breaking Tasks into Manageable Chunks

You know that feeling when **progress** feels like it's moving at a snail's pace? Yeah, me too. But guess what? Breaking **tasks** into bite-sized parts can be a game-changer for fighting off the urge to delay. Think of it as that little dose of satisfaction when you scratch an item off a to-do list. Feels good, right? Even small victories count and can pave the way for even bigger ones. When you can see tangible progress, it gives you a motivational boost to keep going.

So, how do you tackle those gigantic **projects** without feeling overwhelmed? Enter the Work Breakdown Structure, or WBS for short. It's not as complicated as it sounds. Imagine you have this huge task, like planning a massive event. Rather than seeing it as one enormous mountain to climb, you'd split it into smaller, more manageable hills.

Here's how you can do it:

• Identify the Major Components: Break the project into large sections or components. Think of these as the big chunks that need to be tackled.

• Divide Into Smaller Tasks: Take each major component and divide it into smaller tasks. For instance, if you're planning an event, one chunk might be "venue preparation" and this could be sliced into "finding a venue," "booking it," and "arranging decor."

• Assign Time and Resources: Allocate how much time and what resources you'll need for each small task. This isn't just about task management, but also about not feeling swamped with too much at once.

Voilà! Big, scary project now feels more like a series of short, doable tasks. Simple yet effective.

But let's say even breaking it down still leaves you staring at the list, unsure where to start. This is where the "Swiss cheese" **method** comes in handy. Picture a block of cheese. It's solid, right? But if you take little bites out of it, eventually it's full of holes. Your daunting task is that cheese, and your bites are tiny, manageable actions.

Here's how you can apply it:

• Pick Any Spot and Do a Little Bit: Choose a small part or a simple task and just start. You don't have to follow a logical order. The point is to get moving.

- Take Consistent Small Bites: **Consistency** is key. Doing a little every day can make a huge dent in any project without overwhelming you.

- Keep Things Varied: Switch between tasks if you start feeling bored or stuck. This keeps things fresh and your momentum going.

Using these small bites, you'll find the **task** isn't as intimidating, allowing you to chip away at it bit by bit. Before you know it, you'll look back and see how much **progress** you've made. Just like that wheel of Swiss cheese, full of productive little holes.

So next time you're facing that mountain, think of it more like a series of manageable hills—or better yet, a block of Swiss cheese with plenty of bites taken out. The sense of **achievement** you'll feel won't just help fight off delay, but also give you that push to keep moving forward. You'll be amazed at what you can accomplish.

Accountability Systems for Task Completion

You've probably noticed how it's easier to **show up** at the gym if you've promised a friend you'd be there. Well, the same idea works wonders for beating bad habits like procrastination. By making a social **commitment**, you're tapping into that natural urge to not let others down. It's a clever trick to hold yourself to a task when you're answerable to someone else.

Think about it: when you tell someone you're going to do something, it's way harder to back out. That extra layer of responsibility can be incredibly **motivating**. Whether you're wrapping up a project or sticking to a workout plan, making a public promise can be a game-changer. You can even set specific **deadlines** and milestones to keep yourself on track. And here's the kicker: these commitments don't have to be huge. Even small promises like sending a quick progress update can do the trick.

Now, let's dive into the nuts and bolts of setting up **accountability** partnerships or groups. This can be as simple or as complex as you want. Find a partner whose goals line up with yours—or at least someone busy who gets the struggle. Having someone who's not only clued in on your goals but also actively checking in on your progress is like having a built-in alarm that nudges you to get moving.

Here's a straightforward way to set one up:

• Find a buddy – Look for someone you can count on.

• Set clear expectations – What are you both shooting for? What kind of updates do you expect?

• Schedule check-ins – Regular catch-ups, whether weekly or bi-weekly, help keep you both on the same page.

• Use tools – Apps, shared calendars, or simple message threads can keep you both in the loop.

This way, you've got someone to answer to, which makes putting things off way less tempting.

Ever heard of the "public declaration" technique? It's like making a big announcement to ensure you stick to your guns. You can do this through social media, a blog, or even a group you belong to. The key is to make the declaration in a way that others will notice and (hopefully) ask you about later. It adds that little bit of pressure we sometimes need to get off our butts and start ticking off those items on our to-do lists.

When you go public, you're creating a team of unofficial **cheerleaders**. These are people who'll root for your success or ask you how things are coming along—keeping the pressure on in a positive way. For instance, if you're writing a novel, posting about your progress weekly in a writers' community can push you to keep writing, knowing others are expecting those updates. It's a bit nerve-wracking, but that fear can light a fire under you like nothing else.

So go ahead, tell a friend your goals, set up an accountability group, or shout it from your social media rooftops. These strategies might make **defeating** procrastination so much easier. Transform those intentions into actions, one small step at a time.

Practical Exercise: Procrastination-Busting Challenge

Let's kick things off by **identifying** those top three tasks or projects you always seem to put off. Everyone's got 'em, trust me. Maybe it's that report, decluttering your closet, or finally finishing that book you love but never get around to reading. Take a moment to jot them down.

Got your list? Awesome. Now let's **break** each task into smaller, doable steps. Instead of just 'declutter closet,' think 'sort shirts,' 'organize shoes,' and 'pack away out-of-season clothes.' It's like turning a huge dragon into a few small lizards. To make it even clearer, write down these bite-sized steps and feel how much lighter the load seems already.

But writing this stuff down isn't enough. You need **deadlines** - you know, some fire under your seat! Set a date for each step, and one for the whole task. So 'sort shirts' by Tuesday, 'organize shoes' by Wednesday, and so on. Being specific works wonders. Otherwise, it's all too easy to push things to "later."

Next up, tell someone about these deadlines. Heck, find a buddy who's got their list too, and swap goals. Your goal isn't just your secret - it's public. Kind of like having a gym buddy when you need to scream through that last rep. People do show up for each other.

Ever heard of the "eat that frog" method? It means **tackling** your biggest, ugliest task—the giant frog—first thing each day. Do that for a week and see what happens. Sometimes, once you eat that frog, the rest of your day feels like a breeze.

And speaking of techniques, how about trying the Pomodoro Technique? It's simple but effective. **Work** on one of your small steps for 25 minutes straight, then take a 5-minute break. Repeat this a few times, then take a longer break. These bursts can really cut down on distractions.

Track your progress every day, even the small stuff. See what you accomplished and note any challenges. Didn't stay focused today? No sweat, but jot it down. Had a super productive hour? Great, write that down too. Looking at your progress makes it easier to see what's working and what isn't and adjust accordingly.

Finally, when you look back at the week, take stock of everything. Whether your procrastination monster is now just a common house pet or still a fiery creature, there's always room for tweaks. Maybe the Pomodoro sessions work great, but you struggle with deadlines. **Adjust** your approach and gently wrestle those pesky habits.

Paying attention to your hurdles means you'll get better each time. Sometimes a tweak here or there helps keep you on track. It's all about growing and turning those messy, daunting tasks into steps that lead you closer to the finish line.

Just like that, you've turned procrastination into **progress**. It's not about making a massive change in one go. It's about taking one frog…and eating it at a time. Trust the process, buddy. Keep pushing through, 'cause getting through the junk leads you straight to gold.

In Conclusion

This chapter has armed you with some **essential strategies** to help you conquer procrastination. By grasping why you put things off and learning ways to beat it, you can boost your **productivity** and reach your goals with fewer hiccups. Let's break down the main points in simple terms.

You've delved into the **psychological reasons** behind procrastination, giving you insight into why you often drag your feet. Now, you're equipped to spot your own procrastination patterns, identifying when and why you're likely to hit the snooze button on important tasks.

One key **technique** you've picked up is tackling the toughest task first. The idea is to knock out the most challenging job early, making the rest of your day a breeze. You've also learned the art of breaking big, daunting tasks into bite-sized chunks, making them less intimidating and more manageable.

The chapter highlighted the importance of **accountability partners**. By sharing your goals with someone, you're more likely to stay on track and follow through. It's like having a personal cheerleader in your corner!

These are valuable **tools** to help you manage your time and tasks better. Remember, beating procrastination isn't about drastic changes; it's about taking small, doable steps and being honest with yourself about why you delay tasks. Use what you've learned to make a real difference in your daily life.

You've got the **power** to triumph over procrastination and achieve your dreams! It's all about putting these strategies into action and staying committed to your goals. So, why wait? Start applying these **techniques** today and watch your productivity soar!

Chapter 13: Maintaining Long-Term Self-Discipline

Ever wondered why some people always seem to have it together while others are constantly playing catch-up? It's all about maintaining long-term **self-discipline**. You might be curious how this chapter can shake up your daily grind. Here's a little teaser – it's all about those tiny but **powerful** changes.

I'll walk you through creating **habits** that are built to last. You'll see, it's not just about kicking things off with good intentions; it's about paving a path where those habits become second nature.

Ever feel like you're veering off course? We'll dive into the importance of **checking in** with yourself and making adjustments along the way. This way, you stay on track without feeling like you're stuck in a rut.

Trust me, celebrating **milestones**, no matter how small, keeps the journey fun and fuels your **motivation**. I'm a big believer in giving yourself a pat on the back now and then – it works wonders.

And if there's one thing I want you to take away from this chapter, it's that **learning** never stops. You'll always have room to grow, even when you think you've got it all figured out.

Finally, you'll get to put all this into practice with a **plan** that ties everything together, making long-term self-discipline something you actually look forward to maintaining. Let's jump in and shake up how we handle self-discipline, shall we?

Creating Sustainable Habits

Let's talk about **habit stacking**. It's a way to make new habits stick like glue. Here's the idea: You take an existing habit – something you do every single day without thinking – and you tack a new habit onto it. Like piggybacking. For example, let's say you always make coffee in the morning. You could stack a new habit, like drinking a glass of water, right after you make your coffee. Adding new habits to old ones makes it easier to remember to do them.

But why is this so effective? Well, it uses the **power** of routines you already have. You don't disrupt your day because you're just tweaking what's already there. Think of it like adding a new ornament to your Christmas tree. The tree is already standing and decorated; you're just making it a bit prettier with some extras. So, instead of thinking about forming entirely new habits from scratch, look at what's already part of your routine, and consider where you can add something new.

How about designing these habit chains to make them rock-solid? Here's a trick: start simple. You don't need to overhaul your whole life overnight. If you're looking to be more **disciplined**, pick easy, little things to connect. You could link brushing your teeth to doing a one-minute plank. Or pair your lunch break with a five-minute meditation. Basically, chain actions together to create a sequence that feels natural. Over time, these little promises to yourself add up and strengthen your self-discipline muscle.

Another thing to keep in mind: make your new habits specific and obvious. Vague habits – like "getting fit" – don't cut it. Instead, go for "doing 10 push-ups after brushing my teeth in the morning." See the difference? The clearer and more concrete your intentions, the easier it is for your brain to accept them as part of the **routine**.

Let's chat about something called the "**minimum viable habit**." The idea is to start with the tiniest, easiest version of your new habit. Suppose you want to meditate more. Start by meditating for just one minute a day. Seems silly, but here's the magic – one minute's easy. Your mind doesn't rebel against it. Once you're okay doing it for one minute, you can stretch it to five... maybe ten. Small wins build confidence. And before long, you'll find you're setting aside time for longer sessions like a pro.

Why does this matter? Because starting small avoids overwhelming yourself. Too often, we go all in and burn out. By pulling back and beginning with the smallest achievable goal, you stay **consistent**. Consistency, my friend, is the key to long-term self-discipline. It's not about making massive leaps every day. It's taking small, manageable steps and keeping at it.

To sum it all up: habit stacking, creating habit chains, and using the "minimum viable habit" trick are your secret **weapons** for long-lasting discipline. It's all about making life easier, not harder, with incremental, thoughtful changes. So, find those little habits to stack onto, connect them smartly, and start with the teeniest version possible. Pretty soon, you'll be doing them without even thinking. That's the sweet spot – true, effortless **self-discipline**.

Periodic Self-Assessment and Adjustment

Thinking about your **progress** often helps keep your self-discipline strong for a long time. It's not enough to decide on a goal once and just move forward hoping it all falls into place. It's critical to **check** in on yourself regularly and adjust as needed. Let's face it. We all slip up sometimes. That's why you've gotta spend some quality time reviewing how you're doing and where you can step up your game.

A monthly check-up on your self-discipline is a great starting point. Here's how it works:

Pick a day every month that works for you. Maybe the first Saturday or the last Sunday. Stick to it.

Take a step back and spend an hour or so to reflect. Think about the past month. How did you handle your tasks and **goals**? Did you stick to your plans, or did temptations win more than once?

Rate yourself using simple categories like Work, Health, Relationships, Hobbies. Give yourself a score out of 10 in each one. Were you consistently disciplined at work but slacking on your health goals? Note it down.

Spot patterns. Are there habitual pitfalls? Maybe you notice every weekend you pace around your room instead of working on that big project. Find where you missed the mark and figure out why.

Celebrate wins. It's important to recognize what you did well. If you noticed growth or you hit a personal best when lifting weights, celebrate that! Give yourself credit where it's due.

Make a plan. Write out the steps to tackle those weaker areas next month. Refer to that good ol' calendar for blockers you might face. Adjust your approach to those weak spots.

A terrific tool for this process is what I like to call a "personal SWOT **analysis**." Yeah, sounds straight from the business world. But trust me, apply it here, and it works. Here's how you can whip up your own:

Strengths: What's easier for you? Maybe hitting gym sessions or staying organized at work. Whatever comes naturally, jot it down.

Weaknesses: Be blunt with yourself. Where are you messing up? Could be social media sucking away your time, or giving in to those late-night chip cravings.

Opportunities: What's around you that might help? Think about those workshops you wanted to join, or the body double you can use. Or simply a friend who's great with sticking to things. Use your resources.

Threats: Identify what might derail you. Is it upcoming holiday season interruptions? Or those friends who always invite you out when you've got deadlines? Plan to tackle these obstacles.

By laying this out, you get a clear picture on where your self-discipline stands. Remember, the goal here is about ongoing **progress**. You're not aiming for perfection, but to be better each month than you were the last.

This kind of self-evaluation isn't just a tedious task. It's a foundational **habit**. And just like brushing your teeth or hitting the gym, once you integrate this monthly check, it honestly becomes second nature. Set the date, rate yourself, and use that SWOT to stay on track. Soon enough, you'll notice your self-discipline evolving, and those bad habits fading away. That's the real **treasure**. Keep at it, and watch how things change.

Celebrating Milestones and Progress

Celebrating your milestones and **progress** is crucial. Why? Because recognizing your wins keeps your **motivation** up. It's like giving yourself a pat on the back. Sometimes, you get so caught up in chasing the big goals that you forget to appreciate the small victories along the way. Those small wins? They matter. They build up over time and create a sense of **accomplishment**. It's like planting seeds in a garden. You water them daily, and even if you don't see something sprout immediately, each drop matters. Eventually, you'll see the fruits of your labor. Celebrating those tiny sprouts keeps you going.

So, how do you keep that motivation humming? Set up a **reward** system. But it's gotta fit your goals and what you care about. Imagine this. You've been sticking to a workout routine for a month. That's a big deal. But instead of rewarding yourself with a lazy day, maybe treat yourself to new workout gear or a fun fitness class. You want the reward to feel like an extension of your goal, not a detour. Think about what makes you tick.

Here's a simple method to get you started:

• Define Your Milestone: Get specific. Instead of "lose weight," say, "run for 20 minutes every day for a week."

• Choose a Reward: It should be something you genuinely look forward to. Like a night out, a new book, or a cozy spa day.

• Set Milestones Regularly: Make it a habit to recognize small achievements every month or so, not just yearly.

Using rewards wisely ties your present actions to future goals, providing **incentives** to keep pushing forward.

Another thing. Ever tried **gratitude** journaling? It really helps to boost your appreciation for how far you've come, and the effort you're putting in. Think of it as a snapshot of your journey in terms of progress.

Grab a notebook. Jot down three things you're grateful for every day.

• Acknowledge Small Wins: Write about small victories from your day. Defeated procrastination? Write it down.

- Note Efforts, Not Just Results: Appreciate the effort you made even if it didn't lead to immediate success. Tried a new habit even if you've only succeeded half the week? That effort counts.

- Reflect on Changes: Document changes in your mindset or habits. Becoming more patient with yourself? Note how that shift is helping you go the long way.

Practicing gratitude has a good impact on your mindset and helps keep feelings of frustration or impatience at bay. This reflection can highlight things you might've overlooked in the everyday hustle.

Still, the key is to remain **consistent**. Reward systems, gratitude journaling - none of it will work overnight. They require time and the ability to stick them out, even when it feels pointless. Celebrate consistently, and understand that each step is a move forward. Results aren't always immediate, but they're building a foundation. Milestones celebrated create an environment that motivates sustained discipline as you strive to achieve the big, important goals in your life.

So recognize your victories, whether they're significant events or tiny efforts you put into your day. They all count. They all matter. Keep at it. Appreciate it. Recognize it.

Continuous Learning and Self-Improvement

Let's talk about **deliberate practice**. It's not just about repeating something until you get it right. It's about focusing on the right things to improve. Think about learning guitar. You don't just strum mindlessly; you focus on switching chords until your fingers move seamlessly. The same goes for **self-discipline**. Pick an area to improve and break it into small chunks. If you want to stop hitting snooze, start by not snoozing for one week. Nail that, then move to the next small step, like establishing a morning routine.

Want a guide for your journey? Enter the **personal growth plan**. It's your map to continuous improvement. Start simple: figure out what you want to work on. Maybe it's managing your time better or saying no to distractions. Set clear, small goals. Write them down. Be specific. "Get better at managing time" is too vague; "use a timer to work in 25-minute chunks" is a goal you can track.

List your goals, break them into smaller steps, and track your progress. A notebook or simple app will do. Review your progress regularly. Don't beat yourself up if it's not perfect; just see what's working and what's not, and adjust as needed.

Here's a cool trick – **skill stacking**. It's not about picking random skills; it's about combining new skills to make them more powerful together. Picture this: resisting that chocolate cake takes willpower. Pair that with time management, and soon you're not just avoiding cake, you're sticking to your meal plan. Practice these skills individually first, then start combining them.

The neat thing? As you build up more skills, you'll see how they work together. Setting boundaries helps you manage time better, which helps you resist distractions. Focus on small wins first. Master one thing, then move on to the next, combining what you've learned as you go.

Think of it like Lego bricks. Each **skill** is a brick. The more bricks you collect, the more impressive your creations. But you've got to start small. No one builds a castle out of Lego on the first try.

Working on your self-discipline isn't a one-time project. It's an ongoing challenge, but the good news is, you keep getting better. Each bit of progress makes the next steps easier. It's all about that continuous learning and steady improvement.

Put this all together, and you've got a solid plan. Deliberate practice, a growth plan, and smart skill stacking. It's like building your personal fortress of **self-discipline**. Brick by brick. Skill by skill. Before you know it, you'll be crushing those bad habits and achieving goals without constantly battling self-sabotage. You'll be ready to handle whatever life throws at you with ease.

Ready to take that leap? Start small, focus hard, and keep at it. You'll see progress before you know it. You're on your way to building a rock-solid foundation of **self-discipline** that'll stick with you long-term. Keep pushing forward... you've got this!

Practical Exercise: Long-Term Self-Discipline Plan

Staying **disciplined** over the long haul can be tough, but with a bit of planning, you can set yourself up for success. Let's walk through an exercise to make that happen.

First, figure out your long-term **vision** for self-discipline (1-5 years). Think about where you want to be in a few years. Maybe you see yourself more focused, healthier, or outperforming at work. This vision will guide all your plans. Your future self will thank you.

Next, pinpoint key areas where you want to improve. Break it down—do you need better time management, healthier habits, or more consistent work productivity? Identify these spots so you can work on them.

Set **SMART goals** for each area you want to focus on. SMART stands for Specific, Measurable, Achievable, Relevant, and Time-bound. Instead of hoping to "manage time better," aim for something like, "spend one hour less on your phone each day for three months." Concrete goals mean you know when you've hit the mark.

Make a 90-day **action plan** with specific milestones and habits to build. Here's where you lay out your plans. If you're aiming to cut down screen time, decide on daily limits and weekly reviews. Break everything into manageable chunks so it's not overwhelming. Imagine yourself crossing these off as you go.

Set up a weekly review process to **track** how you're doing and make changes if needed. Keep it simple. Dedicate some time—say Sunday evening—to look back on your week. Did you meet your goals? Can you tweak anything to help you succeed next week? Talk about keeping yourself honest.

Schedule monthly check-ins to see how you're **progressing** overall. On a bigger scale, you'll want to see if you're on track for the long-term. Use your 90-day plan milestones as checkpoints. Adjust if things aren't working out like you planned. It's all part of the process. There's always room for refining.

Plan quarterly "recalibration" sessions to make sure your actions match your long-term goals. This is about the long game. Every three months, sit down and see if what you're doing today is leading you toward that 1-5 year vision. Shift gears if needed, no sweat. Realigning your efforts helps keep that vision alive.

Put your plan into **action**, tweak it as needed, and keep the cycle going for steady **growth**. You've crafted your plan—awesome. Now, time for execution. Start building those habits, ticking off those milestones. If life throws a curveball, adapt your plan. Keep the cycle going. With each loop, you'll find yourself growing and getting closer to your long-term goals.

Simple, right? Okay, maybe not so simple, but definitely doable. The trick lies in consistency, staying motivated, and being willing to adapt when things don't go exactly as planned. Starting with these steps should keep you on track and help you become the disciplined powerhouse you want to be. No more postponing. Let's start making that vision a reality!

In Conclusion

This chapter delves into the **methods** for maintaining long-term self-discipline. By zeroing in on creating sustainable **habits**, regularly assessing progress, celebrating **milestones**, and continuous learning, you can foster **resilience** and consistency. The final part offers a practical guide to creating a long-term self-discipline **plan**.

Key Takeaways

In this chapter, you've discovered:

- The concept of habit stacking and the role of habit chains in building long-term **discipline**

- How regular self-reflection promotes sustained self-discipline

- The importance and impact of celebrating milestones on sustaining **motivation**

- The role of ongoing learning and self-improvement in developing self-discipline

- A practical exercise for setting and achieving long-term self-discipline **goals**

By putting these strategies into action, you can cultivate lasting habits, stay fired up, and keep improving on your self-discipline **journey**. Stick to your guns, keep tabs on your progress, and you'll be well on your way to ongoing success. Remember, Rome wasn't built in a day, so keep at it, and you'll see the results you're after!

To Conclude

The **point** of "The Art of Self-Discipline" is to guide you from your current challenges toward a life of self-control, improved habits, and achieved **goals**. This book aims to provide practical techniques to boost your mental toughness, fend off bad habits, and effectively resist temptations that often lead to self-sabotage.

Here's a recap of the journey you've taken:

You've learned about the psychology and neuroscience behind self-discipline, the role of habits, and managing willpower fatigue. This foundational **knowledge** equips you with an understanding of why these elements are crucial for sustaining self-discipline.

You've delved into building mental toughness, exploring its components, and linking it with emotional intelligence and a growth mindset. Knowing these concepts aids in crafting a more resilient character.

You've focused on identifying bad habits and dismantling their loops involving cues, routines, and rewards. Understanding this cycle enables you to replace negative behaviors with positive alternatives, as reinforced by practical habit **tracking**.

You've dealt with resisting temptations through strategies for impulse control and delayed gratification. By designing your environment for success and practicing exposure and response, you're better equipped to withstand any pull towards distraction.

You've learned about SMART goal-setting and aligning these goals with personal values. By breaking them into actionable steps, you can navigate potential obstacles effectively and lay out a personal goal roadmap.

You've explored time management, involving prioritization techniques, the Pomodoro method for peak productivity, and crafting daily routines that eliminate time-wasters. You now have the tools for optimizing your time for better self-discipline.

You've focused on developing a disciplined **mindset** through cognitive restructuring, positive self-talk, and inspiring perseverance using the 40% rule. Mindset shift journaling reinforces these techniques for long-term success.

You've learned about building resilience and grit, handling life's challenges, recovering from setbacks, and stress management. Engaging in resilience-building activities ensures you never lose sight of your end goal despite setbacks.

You've discovered the role of physical health—nutrition, exercise, and sleep—on your willpower and mental clarity. Integrating these facets into a holistic health plan will improve your overall self-control.

You've explored emotional regulation, recognizing and managing emotional triggers to use your emotions as motivation while boosting your emotional intelligence through directed practice.

You've unpacked productivity techniques such as single-tasking, the two-minute rule, and technological aids. Implementing these practices will streamline your tasks and increase your efficiency.

You've learned about overcoming **procrastination** by understanding its root causes and breaking tasks into manageable chunks with accountability systems to conquer delays and improve task completion rates.

Finally, you've emphasized maintaining long-term discipline by creating sustainable habits, periodic self-assessment, celebrating milestones, and continuing self-improvement.

What's next? Picture yourself empowered by manageable habits, resilient mental toughness, and heightened **productivity**. Once you've implemented these strategies, you're set to reach heights you previously only dreamt of. Imagine smoothly navigating through life's temptations, armed with the tools to turn challenges into victories. Every goal seems closer and every setback more manageable.

Ready to dive deeper? Visit this link to find out more: https://pxl.to/LoganMind

Other Books

To truly **enrich** your journey and maximize your potential growth, it's beneficial to complement your reading experience with insights from other relevant topics in the same realm. While this book has provided you with valuable **strategies** to enhance your self-discipline, you can take your personal **development** even further by exploring additional areas closely related to this subject.

I've authored several other books that either are already available or will be shortly released, each designed to support you on your quest for betterment.

You might consider augmenting the skills gained in this book with highly practical ways to master your **emotions**. Learning how to control and leverage your emotional intelligence lets you handle stress, improve your relationships, and achieve your goals with greater ease.

On top of emotional methods, you could grasp the techniques to build and maintain high **self-esteem**. Empower yourself with the confidence to take bold steps forward without fear of failure.

Finally, you might want to enhance your cognitive capabilities via **brain training**. A sharp, adaptable mind elevates you above challenges, ensuring you stay one step ahead in every aspect of life.

The **synergies** across these books provide a wider lens through which you can view and tackle your personal improvement journey.

Check out all my books and contacts here:

https://pxl.to/LoganMind

Help Me!

When you **support** an independent author, you're helping to bring a **dream** to life.

If you found my book fulfilling, please take a moment to leave an **honest** review by visiting the link below. Your **feedback** is invaluable, and it helps me improve and reach more readers just like you.

You can leave a review if you're satisfied. If you have any suggestions for improvements, feel free to reach out via email through the same link.

Alternatively, you can scan the **QR code** and find the link after you select your book.

It only takes a few seconds, but letting your voice be heard has a **massive** impact on an author's journey.

Visit this link to leave your feedback:

https://pxl.to/6-taos-lm-review

Your support means the **world** to me!

Join my Review Team!

Thank you so much for reading my book! Your support means the **world** to me. I'm thrilled to invite you to join my **Review Team**. As a team member, you'll get **free** copies of my upcoming releases in exchange for your honest and valuable **feedback**. This would greatly help me deliver better **content** to readers like you.

If you're an avid **reader**, joining the team is simple and rewarding.

Here's how you can hop on board:

- Click on the link or scan the QR code provided.

- Once the page opens, click on my book cover.# Download Your Free Book!

As a way of saying thanks for your purchase, I'm offering the book **Emotional Intelligence** for Social Success for FREE to you, my reader.

Inside the book, you'll **discover** a wealth of valuable information. You'll learn techniques to **improve** your social interactions and strategies to **manage** your emotions effectively. You'll also pick up tips on developing **empathy** and understanding, gain insights into building stronger **relationships**, and learn methods to handle social **challenges** with ease.

If you want to **boost** your emotional intelligence and succeed in social environments, make sure to grab this free book. It's a game-changer!

To get instant **access**, just head over to:

https://pxl.to/loganmindfreebook

Don't miss out on this opportunity to enhance your social skills and emotional intelligence. Get your free copy now!

www.ingramcontent.com/pod-product-compliance
Lightning Source LLC
Chambersburg PA
CBHW050235120526
44590CB00016B/2100